David Ames Wells, Frédéric Bastiat

Essays on Political Economy

David Ames Wells, Frédéric Bastiat

Essays on Political Economy

ISBN/EAN: 9783744645133

Printed in Europe, USA, Canada, Australia, Japan

Cover: Foto ©Suzi / pixelio.de

More available books at **www.hansebooks.com**

ESSAYS

ON

POLITICAL ECONOMY

BY
FREDERICK BASTIAT

English Translation Revised, with Notes
BY
DAVID A. WELLS

"*Moins on sait, moins on doute; moins on a découvert, moins on voit ce qui reste à découvrir.*"—(The less one knows, the less one doubts; the less one discovers, the less he will see what there is to discover.)—TURGOT.

NEW YORK
G. P. PUTNAM'S SONS
182 FIFTH AVENUE
1877

PREFACE BY THE AMERICAN EDITOR.

POLITICAL ECONOMY, in the opinion of most men, is but the expression or name for something that is typically dry, wearisome, and unpractical. Owing to the sad record of the follies of legislators, and governments, of which it especially takes cognizance, and to the unfavorable conclusions respecting human development to which some of its investigators and teachers have been led, it has also received the name of "*The Dismal Science.*"

But if political economy has become popularly invested with such attributes, and has been stigmatized with a bad name, it is certainly because of the methods and manner in which its precepts and principles have been taught, rather than because the science itself is either repulsive in theory or unprofitable in its practical application. For political economy, in truth, is but the history and discussion of the results of the experience of mankind in getting a living, and in securing that degree of material abundance which will admit of leisure, without which there can be no attainments in knowledge. And the all-absorbing feeling of interest which invariably takes possession of those who through study have come to fully appreciate the nature of the science, centers in the hope and belief that through the determination and dissemination of the principles deducible from this experience of mankind, toil, hereafter, to the masses, will be made lighter, justice rendered more certain, comfort increased, and abundance be made greater.

In further illustration of these propositions, attention is asked to the nature of the work performed by the two men, who, more than any others, may be considered as having founded, during the last century, the science of modern political economy, namely, Turgot and Adam Smith. The former became finance minister of France in 1774, under Louis XVI., shortly after the death of Louis XV. He found France, and in fact all Europe, steeped in poverty and threatened with future calamities, not because the country was deficient in natural resources or the people unwilling to labor, but because through lack of any appreciation or understanding of the most simple economic laws and principles, the governmental authorities had so multiplied taxes, monopolized trade, and restricted commerce, that production was everywhere carried on at the minimum of profit, accumulation prevented, and distribution so impeded that the people in one province were sometimes allowed to starve, while in an adjoining department there was a surplus seeking a market. Turgot attempted reform by practically applying and carrying out the elementary principles which are now embodied as axioms in every modern treatise on political economy. By royal edict issued in January, 1776, he made it lawful, for the first time in France, for any person, man or woman, to follow without hindrance any craft or profession; he abolished all the privileges and monopolies of all the guilds, corporations, and trading companies of the kingdom; he removed restrictions on trade at home, and on commerce with foreign nations; and in place of a system of diffused, inquisitorial, infinitesimal taxes, endeavored to concentrate taxation on a comparatively few objects. The following extract from this celebrated edict (made in the name of the king, but written by Turgot), which it is believed has never before been translated into English, further illustrates what political economy was understood to be by this one of the acknowledged founders of the science :—

"It has come to be a popular notion that the right to labor is a matter of royal prerogative; something that the ruler (State) is able to sell; something which the subject ought to buy; and therefore that the sale of grants and privileges to labor, to produce, and to exchange ought to be made a source of revenue to the State." We hasten to repudiate any such principle. God in giving to man wants, rendered it necessary that he should have property. The right to labor is not only the property of all men, but it is the first, the most sacred, and the most imprescribable of all property. We therefore regard it is as the first obligation on our justice, and as an act most worthy of our beneficence, to free all our subjects from every restriction on this most inalienable right of humanity. We therefore abrogate every arbitrary institution that does not permit the poor to freely enjoy the fruits of their labor; which tramples down the sex whose weakness gives it more of wants and less of resources, and which in condemning woman to poverty and idleness promotes immorality and debauchery; which extinguishes emulation in industry, and renders useless the talent of those who are excluded from trade associations; which deprives the State of the industry, the trade, and the products of foreigners; which retards the progress of the arts; and finally, which gives facility to members of corporations to so intrigue among themselves as to force those who are poor to submit to the will of the rich, and so become the instruments of monoply and the supporters of schemes, the sole effect of which is to enable a few to enjoy more than their rightful proportion of these commodities which are essential to the subsistence and comfort of the masses."

This edict, which was little else than the enunciation of the modern non-interference theory of government with production and distribution, was characterized at the time by Voltaire as the greattest single step ever taken in civilization. It did not, however, succeed, because popular ignorance and the interests of individuals, as contradistinguished from the interests of the masses, which undoubtedly regarded then (as they regard now) the views of students of economic laws as dry and unpractical, soon effected the revocation of the edict. But had it been maintained, the French revolution of 1789—certainly with its "reign of terror"—would probably never have occurred.

Consider also the influence of the work performed by that other great political economist, Adam Smith, as embodied in his "Inquiry into the Nature and Causes of the Wealth of Nations." One hundred years after the publication of this book, the judgment of an acknowledged financial authority,* after a thorough investigation of the whole subject was, that it has "*caused more money to be made, and prevented more money from being lost, than the writings of any other author;*" while the opinion of another,† not less qualified to pass judgment, is, that the claim to merit of Adam Smith's teachings was not "that it made a number of rich men richer than they were before, but that it invented a beneficial and blessed secret of mitigating the labor of those who were in hard and bitter circumstances, giving comfort and even reasonable abundance, not to scores, or hundreds, or thousands, but to millions to whom before life was a burden."

London Economist, June, 1876.   † Hon. W. E. Gladstone.

But if political economy is thus as practical and beneficent in its teaching and application as historical results and the concurrent testimony of those best qualified to judge agree that it has been and is; if it tends to throw light on what all mankind are especially interested in doing, namely, improving their material welfare, it would seem that its study ought to be a matter of special interest to all, and its principles and propositions anything but dry and uninteresting. Of course, in the presentation of its truths and results there is a wide difference in the capacity of those who by study and investigation have acquired a rightful authority to teach. The possession of large knowledge and the power of readily and attractively communicating it, are not often happily united in one and the same person; but in the case of the eminent Frenchman, M. Frederick Bastiat (born 1801, died in 1850), these two qualities were so conjoined that his expositions and illustrations of politico-economic topics are acknowledged to be more lucid and convincing than those of almost any other author. He foresaw that a knowledge of the fundamental principles of political economy diffused among the masses was the only "safeguard of democracy," and the surest guarantee for the continuation and prosperity of all forms of government that are based on extended or universal suffrage. He had the most earnest convictions of the truth of a proposition laid down by the late Harriet Martineau, more than forty years ago, in the preface to one of her popular essays, that "if it concerns rulers that their measures should be wise; if it concerns the wealthy that their property should be secure, the middling classes that their industry should be rewarded, the poor that their hardships should be redressed, it concerns all that political economy should be understood." And with this foresight, and with these convictions, M. Bastiat especially devoted himself to the presentation and elucidation of those questions in political economy which are of the utmost importance—because they intimately concern the welfare of the masses—that the masses should thoroughly understand; and the lack of which understanding has not only already occasioned serious troubles in almost every civilized community, but threatens still greater evil for the future. Another great merit of his writings is, that they are almost wholly free from a blemish that characterizes a large number of the works on political economy that were designed to be popular, namely, the discussion of controverted points and niceties, and references to books and authors that have preceded, but which are little known, or not accessible to the majority of readers.

This little volume is made up of a selection from the essays of M. Bastiat that have in a high degree these popular and attractive characteristics; such as a presentation of *the nature of capital and interest,* and the relation of the two; a discussion, under the title "*That which is Seen, and that which is not Seen,*" of the evils that always result from limiting consideration of the effect of an economic law, tax, or institution to its immediate visible influence and ignoring its ultimate consequences, introducing in so doing the illustration which has passed into many languages of the "*Broken Window.*" Also the question of "*What is Government?*" "*What is Money?*" and the nature, object, and function of what is popularly and generally termed "*The Law,*" without reference to any particular code or statute. So acceptable, indeed, have these short selected essays proved to the public, that repeated editions of them have been published in France, Belgium, Germany, Italy, England, and the United States; and all that the Editor has had to do with the present American edition has been to revise the previous English translation, which was exceedingly imperfect, and in some instances absolutely without meaning. Where the text, which was originally written to meet the condition of affairs in France, at the time of the overthrow of the monarchy and the establishment of the republic in 1848, could be changed verbally with advantage to meet the different condition of men, laws, and things at present existing in the United States, such changes have been made;—English names being substituted for French ones, dollars and cents in place of francs and sous, and the like. A few notes pertinent to the subject-matter of the text, and drawn mainly from the recent economic experience of the United States, have also been added.

Finally, as no pecuniary advantage whatever accrues to the Editor from any revision or republication of these essays, he feels at liberty to commend them to all friends of economic studies and reforms in the United States, and to ask their co-operation in extending their circulation among the people.

DAVID A. WELLS.

NORWICH, CONN., *February*, 1877.

CONTENTS.

CAPITAL AND INTEREST.

INTRODUCTION	1
OUGHT CAPITAL TO PRODUCE INTEREST?	8
WHAT IS CAPITAL?	23
THE SACK OF CORN	24
THE HOUSE	28
THE PLANE	30
WHAT REGULATES INTEREST?	48

THAT WHICH IS SEEN, AND THAT WHICH IS NOT SEEN ... 70

THE BROKEN WINDOW	72
THE DISBANDING OF TROOPS	77
TAXES	82
THEATRES, FINE ARTS	87
PUBLIC WORKS	96
THE MIDDLE-MEN	100
RESTRICTIONS	109
MACHINERY	117

CREDIT	127
ALGERIA	134
FRUGALITY AND LUXURY	141
HE WHO HAS A RIGHT TO LABOR HAS A RIGHT TO THE PROFIT OF LABOR	150
GOVERNMENT	154
WHAT IS MONEY?	174
THE LAW	221

CAPITAL AND INTEREST.

INTRODUCTION.

My object in this treatise is to examine into the real nature of the Interest of Capital, for the purpose of proving that it is lawful, and explaining why it should be perpetual. This may appear singular, and yet, I confess, I am more afraid I may weary the reader by a series of mere truisms. But it is no easy matter to avoid this danger, when the facts with which we have to deal are known to every one by personal, familiar, and daily experience.

But, then, you will say, "What is the use of this treatise? Why explain what everybody knows?"

But, although this problem appears at first sight so very simple, there is more in it than you might suppose. I shall endeavor to prove this by an example. Thomas lends an instrument of labor to-day, which will be entirely destroyed in a week, yet the capital will not produce the less interest to Thomas or his heirs, through all eternity. Reader, can you honestly say that you understand the reason of this?

It would be a waste of time to seek any satisfactory explanation from the writings of economists. They have not thrown much light upon the reasons of the existence of interest. For this they are not to be blamed; for at the time they wrote, its lawfulness was not called in question. Now, however, times are altered; the case is different. Men, who consider themselves to be in advance of their age, have organized an active crusade against capital and interest; it is the productiveness of capital which they are attacking; not certain abuses in the administration of it, but the principle itself.

Some years ago a journal was established in Paris by M. Proudhon, especially to promote this crusade, which for a time is reported to have had a very large circulation. The first number that was issued contained the following declaration of its principles:—" The productiveness of capital, which is condemned by Christianity under the name of usury, is the true cause of misery, the true origin of destitution, the eternal obstacle to the establishment of a true Republic."

Another French journal, *La Ruche Populaire*, also thus expresses its views on this subject:— " But above all, labor ought to be free; that is, it ought to be organized in such a manner *that money-lenders and owners or controllers of capital should not be paid* for granting the opportunity to labor, and for which privilege they charge as high a price as possible. The only thought that I notice here, is that expressed by the words in the italics, which imply a denial of the right to take interest.

A noted leader among the French Socialists, M. Thoré, also thus expresses himself:—

"The revolution will always have to be recommenced, so long as we occupy ourselves with consequences only, without having the logic or the courage to attack the principle itself. This principle is capital, false property, interest, and usury, which by old custom is made to weigh upon labor.

"Ever since the aristocrats invented the incredible fiction, *that capital possesses the power of reproducing itself*, the workers have been at the mercy of the idle.

"At the end of a year, will you find an additional dollar in a bag of one hundred dollars? At the end of fourteen years will your dollars have doubled in your bag?

"Will a work of industry or of skill produce another, at the end of fourteen years?

"Let us begin, then, by demolishing this fatal fiction."

I have quoted the above, merely for the sake of establishing the fact that many persons consider the productiveness of capital a false, a fatal, and an iniquitous principle.* But quotations are

---

* In this essay, written for his countrymen, M. Bastiat quotes exclusively, as was natural, from French writers, for the purpose of illustrating the views of those who maintain that the loan of capital for interest or hire is iniquitous from a moral point of view, and economically considered unprofitable to the people collectively. But quotations of a similar character might equally well have been made from English and American writers, who in some instances are men who have attained to no little reputation. Thus, for example, John Ruskin, the well-known English art critic, in his *Fors Clavigera*, thus reasons respecting "the immoral nature and injurious effects" of the taking of interest. "Usury," he says, "is properly the taking of money for the loan or use of anything (over and above what pays for wear and tear), such use involving no care or labor on the part of the lender. It includes all investments of capital whatsoever, returning 'dividends,' as distinguished from labor wages or profits. Thus anybody who works on a railroad as plate-layer or stoker has a right to wages for his work; and any inspector of wheels or rails has a right to payment for such inspection; but idle persons who have only paid a hundred pounds towards the road-making, have a right to the return of the hundred pounds—and no more. If they take a farthing more, they are usurers. They may take fifty pounds for two years, twenty-five for four, five for twenty, or one for a hundred. But the first farthing they take more than their hundred, be it sooner or later, is usury.

"Again, when we build a house, and let it, we have a right to as much rent as will return us the wages of our labor, and superfluous; it is well known that large numbers of poor people attribute their poverty to what they call the *tyranny of capital;* meaning thereby the unwillingness of the owners of capi-

---

the sum of our outlay. If, as in ordinary cases, not laboring with our hands or head, we have simply paid—say one thousand pounds—to get the house built, we have a right to the one thousand pounds back again at once, if we sell it ; or, if we let it, to five hundred pounds rent during two years, or one hundred pounds rent during ten years or ten pounds rent during a hundred years. But if, sooner or later, we take a pound more than the thousand, we are usurers.

"And thus in all other possible or conceivable cases, the moment our capital is 'increased' by having lent it, be it but in the estimation of a hair; that hair's-breadth of increase is usury, just as much as stealing a farthing is theft, no less than stealing a million.

"But usury is worse than theft, in so far as it is obtained either by deceiving people or distressing them ; generally by both ; and finally by deceiving the usurer himself, who comes to think that usury is a real increase, and that money can grow of money ; whereas all usury is increase to one person only by decrease to another; and every grain of calculated Increment to the rich is balanced by its mathematical equivalent of Decrement to the poor." And again: "We need not fear our power of becoming good Christians yet, if we will ; so only that we understand, finally and utterly, that all gain, increase, interest, or whatever else you call it or think it, to the lender of capital, is loss, decrease, and disinterest to the borrower of capital. Every farthing we, who lend the tool, make, the borrower of the tool loses. And all the idiotical calculations of what money comes to, in so tal to allow others to use it without security for its safe return and compensation for its use.

I believe there is not a man in the world, who is aware of the whole importance of this question : "Is the interest of capital natural, just, and lawful, and as useful to the borrower who pays, as to the lender who receives?"

You answer, No; I answer, Yes. Then we differ entirely; but it is of the utmost importance

---

many years, simply ignore the debit side of the book, on which the Laborer's Deficit is precisely equal to the Capitalist's Efficit. I saw an estimate made by some blockhead in an American paper, the other day, of the weight of gold which a hundred years' 'interest' on such and such funds would load the earth with ! Not even of wealth in that solid form, could the poor wretch perceive so much of the truth as that the gold he put on the earth above, he must dig out of the earth below ! But the mischief in real life is far deeper on the negative side, than the good on the positive. The debt of the borrower loads his heart, cramps his hands, and dulls his labor. The gain of the lender hardens his heart, fouls his brain, and puts every means of mischief into his otherwise clumsy and artless hands."

As an illustration of similar views of American origin, a pamphlet on Labor Reform, by John T. Campbell, of Indiana, published in 1872, and which has attained considerable popularity and circulation, thus commences a chapter *on the causes affecting the distribution of wealth:*

" What, then, are the means used by which wealth which labor produces is transferred to the possession of the non-producing few? It is simply an instrument of refined robbery. It is money and its interest."

to discover which of us is in the right, otherwise we shall incur the danger of making a false solution of the question, a matter of opinion. If the error is on my side, however, the evil would not be so great. It must be inferred that I know nothing about the true interests of the masses, or the march of human progress; and that all my arguments are but as so many grains of sand, by which the car of the revolution will certainly not be arrested.

But if, on the contrary, men like Proudhon and Thoré in France (John Ruskin in England, and others in the United States) are deceiving themselves, it follows that they are leading the people astray—that they are showing them evil where it does not exist; and thus giving a false direction to their ideas, to their antipathies, to their dislikes, and to their attacks. It follows that the misguided people are rushing into a horrible and absurd struggle, in which victory would be more fatal than defeat; since, according to this supposition, the result would be the realization of universal evils, the destruction of every means of emancipation, the consummation of its own misery.

This is just what M. Proudhon has acknowledged, with perfect good faith. "The foundation stone," he told me, "of my system is the *gratui-*

tousness of credit. If I am mistaken in this, Socialism is a vain dream." I add, it is a dream, in which the people are tearing themselves to pieces. Will it, therefore, be a cause for surprise, if, when they awake, they find themselves mangled and bleeding? Such a danger as this is enough to justify me fully, if, in the course of the discussion, I allow myself to be led into some trivialities and some prolixity.

OUGHT CAPITAL TO PRODUCE INTEREST?

I address this treatise to working men, more especially to those who have enrolled themselves under the banner of Socialist democracy. I proceed to consider these two questions:—

1st. Is it consistent with the nature of things, and with justice, that capital should produce interest?

2d. Is it consistent with the nature of things, and with justice, that the interest of capital should be perpetual?

The working men everywhere will certainly acknowledge that a more important subject could not be discussed.

Since the world began, it has been allowed, at least in part, that capital ought to produce interest. But latterly it has been affirmed that herein lies the very social error which is the cause of pauperism and inequality. It is, therefore, very essential to know now on what ground we stand.

For if levying interest from capital is a sin, the workers have a right to revolt against social order, as it exists. It is in vain to tell them that they ought to have recourse to legal and pacific means: it would be a hypocritical recommendation. When on the one side there is a strong man, poor, and a victim of robbery—on the other, a weak man, but rich, and a robber—it is singular enough that we should say to the former, with a hope of persuading him, "Wait till your oppressor voluntarily renounces oppression, or till it shall cease of itself." This cannot be; and those who tell us that capital is by nature unproductive, ought to know that they are provoking a terrible and disastrous struggle.

If, on the contrary, the interest of capital is natural, lawful, consistent with the general good, as favorable to the borrower as to the lender, the economists who deny it, the writers who grieve over this pretended social wound, are leading the workmen into a senseless and unjust effort which can have no other issue than the misfortune of all. In fact, they are arming labor against capital. So much the better, if these two powers are really antagonistic; and may the struggle soon be ended! But, if they are in harmony, the struggle is the greatest evil which can be inflicted on society. You see, then, workmen, that there is not a more important question than this:—"Is the interest of capital rightful or not?" In the former case, you must immediately renounce the struggle to which you are being urged; in the second, you must carry it on bravely, and to the end.

Productiveness of capital—perpetuity of interest. These are difficult questions. I must endeavor to make myself clear. And for that purpose I shall have recourse to example rather than to demonstration; or rather, I shall place the demonstration in the example. I begin by acknowledging that, at first sight, it may appear strange that capital should pretend to a remuneration, and above all to a perpetual remuneration. You will say, "Here are two men. One of them works from morning till night, from one year's end to another; and if he consumes all which he has gained, even by superior energy, he remains poor. When Christmas comes he is in no better condition than he was at the beginning of the year, and has no other prospect but to begin again. The other man does nothing, either with his hands or his head; or at least, if he makes use of them at all, it is only for his own pleasure; it is allowable for him to do nothing, for he has an income. He does not work, yet he lives well; he has everything in abundance; delicate dishes, sumptuous furniture, elegant equipages; nay, he even consumes, daily, things which the workers have been obliged to produce by the sweat of their brow, for these things do not make themselves; and, as far as he is concerned, he has had no hand in their production. It is the workmen who have caused this corn to grow, elaborated this furniture, woven these carpets; it is our wives and daughters who have spun, cut-out, sewed, and embroidered these stuffs. We work, then, for him and for ourselves; for him first, and then for ourselves, if there is anything left. But here is something more striking still. If the former of these two men, the worker, consumes within the year any profit which may have been left him in that year, he is always at the point from which he started, and his destiny condemns him to move incessantly in a perpetual circle, and in a monotony of exertion. Labor, then, is rewarded only once. But if the other, the 'gentleman,' consumes his yearly income in the year, he has, the year after, in those which follow, and through all eternity, an income always equal, inexhaustible, *perpetual.* Capital, then, is remunerated, not only once or twice, but an indefinite number of times! So that, at the end of a hundred years, a family which has placed 20,000 francs,* at five per cent. will have had 100,000 francs; and this will not prevent from having 100,000 francs more in the following century. In other words, for 20,000 francs, which represents its labor, it will have levied, in two centuries, a tenfold value on the labor of others. In this social arrangement is there not a monstrous evil to be reformed? And this is not all. If it should please this family to curtail its enjoyments a little—to spend, for example, only 900 francs, instead of 1,000—it may, without any labor, without any other trouble beyond that of investing 100 francs a year, increase its capital and its income in such rapid progression that he will soon be in a position to consume as much as a hundred families of industrious workmen. Does not all this go to prove that society itself has in its bosom a hideous cancer, which ought to be eradicated at the risk of some temporary suffering?"

These are, it appears to me, the sad and irritating reflections which must be excited in your minds by the active and superficial crusade which is being carried on against capital and interest. On the other hand, there are moments in which, I am convinced, doubts are awakened in your

---

* A franc is 19.3 cents of our money.

minds, and scruples in your conscience. You say to yourselves sometimes: "But to assert that capital ought not to produce interest, is to say that he who has created instruments of labor, or materials, or provisions of any kind, ought to yield them up without compensation. Is that just? And then, if it is so, who would lend these instruments, these materials, these provisions? who would take care of them? who even would create them? Every one would consume his proportion, and the human race would not advance a step. Capital would be no longer accumulated, since there would be no interest in accumulating it. It would become exceedingly scarce. This would be a most singular step for the obtaining of loans gratuitously! A singular means of improving the condition of borrowers, to make it impossible for them to borrow at any price! What would become of labor itself? for there will be no money advanced, and not one single kind of labor can be mentioned, not even the chase, which can be pursued without capital of some kind. And, as for ourselves, what would become of us? What! we are not to be allowed to borrow, in order to work in the prime of life, nor to lend, that we may enjoy repose in its decline? The law will rob us of the prospect of laying by a little property, because it will prevent us from gaining any advantage from it. It will deprive us of all stimulus to save at the present time, and of all hope of repose for the future. It is useless to exhaust ourselves with fatigue; we must abandon the idea of leaving our sons and daughters a little property, since the new views render it useless, for we should become traffickers in the toil of men if we were to lend it on interest. Alas! the world which these persons would open before us, as an imaginary good, is still more dreary and desolate than that which they condemn, for hope, at any rate, is not banished from the latter." Thus, in all respects, and in every point of view, the question is a serious one. Let us hasten to arrive at a solution.

The French civil code has a chapter entitled, "On the manner of transmitting property." When a man by his labor has made some useful things—in other words, when he has created a *value*—it can only pass into the hands of another by one of the following modes:—*as a gift, by the right of inheritance, by exchange, loan, or theft*. One word upon each of these, except the last, although it plays a greater part in the world than we may think. A *gift* needs no definition. It is essentially voluntary and spontaneous. It depends exclusively upon the giver, and the receiver cannot be said to have any right to it. Without a doubt, morality and religion make it a duty for men, especially the rich, to deprive themselves voluntarily of that which they possess, in favor of their less fortunate brethren. But this is an entirely moral obligation. If it were to be asserted on principle, admitted in practice, sanctioned by law, that every man has a right to the property of another, the gift would have no merit—charity and gratitude would be no longer virtues. Besides, such a doctrine would suddenly and universally arrest labor and production, as severe cold congeals water and suspends animation; for who would work if there was no longer to be any connection between labor and the satisfying of our wants? Political economy has not treated of gifts. It has hence been concluded that it disowns them, and that it is therefore a science devoid of heart. This is a ridiculous accusation. That science which treats of the laws resulting from the *reciprocity of services* had no business to inquire into the consequences of generosity with respect to him who receives, nor into its effects, perhaps still more precious, on him who gives. Such considerations belong evidently to the science of morals. We must allow the sciences to have limits; above all, we must not accuse them of denying or undervaluing what they look upon as foreign to their department.

The *right of inheritance*, against which so much has been objected of late, is one of the forms of gift, and assuredly the most natural of all. That which a man has produced, he may consume, exchange, or give. What can be more natural than that he should give it to his children? It is this power, more than any other, which inspires him with courage to labor and to save. Do you know why the principle of right of inheritance is thus called in question? Because it is imagined that the property thus transmitted is plundered from the masses. This is a fatal error. Political economy demonstrates, in the most peremptory manner, that all value produced is a creation which does no harm to any person whatever. For that reason it may be consumed, and, still more, transmitted, without hurting any one; but I shall not pursue these reflections, which do not belong to the subject.

Exchange is the principal department of political economy, because it is by far the most frequent method of transmitting property, according to the free and voluntary acquiescence in the laws and effects of which this science treats.

Properly speaking, exchange is the reciprocity of services. The parties say between themselves, "Give me this, and I will give you that;" or, "Do this for me, and I will do that for you." It is well to remark (for this will throw a new light on the notion of value) that the second form is always implied in the first. When it is said, "Do this for me, and I will do that for you," an exchange of service for service is proposed. Again, when it is said, "Give me this, and I will give you that," it is the same as saying, "I yield to you what I have done, yield to me what you have done." The labor is past, instead of present; but the exchange is not the less governed by the comparative valuation of the two services; so that it is quite correct to say that the principle of *value* is in the services rendered and received on account of the productions exchanged, rather than in the productions themselves.

In reality, services are scarcely ever exchanged directly. There is a medium, which is termed *money*. Paul has completed a coat, for which he wishes to receive a little bread, a little wine, a little oil, a visit from a doctor, a ticket for the play, etc. The exchange cannot be effected in kind, so what does Paul do? He first exchanges his coat for some money, which is called *selling;* then he exchanges this money again for the things which he wants, which is called *purchasing;* and now, only, has the reciprocity of service completed its circuit; now, only, the labor and the compensation are balanced in the same individual,—" I have done this for society, it has done that for me." In a word, it is only now that the exchange is actually accomplished. Thus, nothing can be more correct than this observation of J. B. Say:—" Since the introduction of money, every exchange is resolved into two elements, *sale* and *purchase*. It is the reunion of these two elements which renders the exchange complete."

We must remark, also, that the constant appearance of money in every exchange has overturned and misled all our ideas: men have ended in thinking that money was true riches, and that to multiply it was to multiply services and products. Hence the protective system; hence paper money; hence the celebrated aphorism, "What one gains the other loses;" and of the errors which have impoverished the earth, and imbrued it with blood.* After much investigation it has been found, that in order to make the two services exchanged of equivalent value, and in order to render the exchange *equitable*, the best means was to allow it to be free. However plausible, at first sight, the intervention of the State might be, it was soon perceived that it is always oppressive to one or other of the contracting

---

* This error M. Bastiat afterward specially combated and exposed in a pamphlet, entitled *Cursed Money*.

parties. When we look into these subjects, we are always compelled to reason upon this maxim, that *equal value* results from liberty. We have, in fact, no other means of knowing whether, at a given moment, two services are of the same value, but that of examining whether they can be readily and freely exchanged. Allow the State, which is the same thing as force, to interfere on one side or the other, and from that moment all the means of appreciation will be complicated and entangled, instead of becoming clear. It ought to be the part of the State to prevent, and, above all, to repress artifice and fraud; that is, to secure liberty, and not to violate it. I have enlarged a little upon exchange, although loan is my principal object: my excuse is, that I conceive that there is in a loan an actual exchange, an actual service rendered by the lender, and which makes the borrower liable to an equivalent service,—two services, whose comparative value can only be appreciated, like that of all possible services, by freedom. Now, if it is so, the perfect rightfulness of what is called house-rent, farm-rent, interest, will be explained and understood. Let us consider what is involved in a *loan*.

Suppose two men exchange two services or two objects, whose equal value is beyond all dispute. Suppose, for example, Peter says to Paul, " Give me ten ten-cent pieces, I will give you a silver dollar." We cannot imagine an equal value more unquestionable. When the bargain is made, neither party has any claim upon the other. The exchanged services are equal. Then it follows, that if one of the parties wishes to introduce into the bargain an additional clause, advantageous to himself, but unfavorable to the other party, he must agree to a second clause, which shall reestablish the equilibrium, and the law of justice. It would be absurd to deny the justice of a second clause of compensation. This granted, we will suppose that Peter, after having said to Paul, "Give me ten ten-cent pieces, I will give you a dollar," adds, "You shall give me the ten ten-cent pieces *now*, and I will give you the silver dollar *in a year;*" it is very evident that this new proposition alters the claims and advantages of the bargain; that it alters the proportion of the two services. Does it not appear plainly enough, in fact, that Peter asks of Paul a new and an additional service; one of a different kind? Is it not as if he had said, "Render me the service of allowing me to use for my profit, for a year, the dollar which belongs to you, and which you might have used for yourself?" And what good reason have you to maintain that Paul is bound to render this especial service gratuitously; that he has no right to demand anything more in consequence of this requisition; that the State ought to interfere to force him to submit? Is it not incomprehensible that the economist, who preaches such a doctrine to the people, can reconcile it with his principle of *the reciprocity of service?* Here I have introduced money; I have been led to do so by a desire to place, side by side, two objects of exchange, of a perfect and indisputable equality of value. I was anxious to be prepared for objections; but, on the other hand, my demonstration would have been more striking still, if I had illustrated my principle by an agreement for exchanging of services or commodities directly.

Suppose, for example, a house and a vessel of a value so perfectly equal that their proprietors are disposed to exchange them even-handed, without excess or abatement. In fact let the bargain be settled by a lawyer. At the moment of each taking possession, the ship-owner says to the house-owner, "Very well; the transaction is completed, and nothing can prove its perfect equity better than our free and voluntary consent. Our conditions thus fixed, I will propose to you a little practical modification. You shall let me have your house to-day, but I will not put you in possession of my ship for a year; and the reason I make this demand of you is, that, during this year of *delay*, I wish to use the vessel." That we may not be embarrassed by considerations relative to the deterioration of the thing lent, I will suppose the ship-owner to add, "I will engage, at the end of the year, to hand over to you the vessel in the state in which it is to-day." I ask of every candid man, if the house-owner has not a right to answer, "The new clause which you propose entirely alters the proportion or the equal value of the exchanged services. By it I shall be deprived, for the space of a year, both at once of my house and of your vessel. By it you will make use of both. If, in the absence of this clause, the bargain was just, for the same reason the clause is injurious to me. It stipulates for a loss to me, and a gain to you. You are requiring of me a new service; I have a right to refuse, or to require of you, as a compensation, an equivalent service." If the parties are agreed upon this compensation, the principle of which is incontestable, we can easily distinguish two transactions in one, two exchanges of service in one. First, there is the exchange of the house for the vessel; after this, there is the delay granted by one of the parties, and the compensation corresponding to this delay yielded by the other. These two new services take the generic and abstract names of *credit* and *interest*. But names do not change the nature of things; and I defy any one to disprove that there exists here, when all is done, a service for a service, or a reciprocity of services. To say that one of these services does not challenge the other, to say that the first ought to be rendered gratuitously, without injustice, is to say that injustice consists in the reciprocity of service,—that justice consists in one of the parties giving and not receiving, which is a contradiction in terms.

But, to give an idea of interest and its mechanism, allow me to make use of two or three anecdotes. But, first, I must say a few words upon capital.

WHAT IS CAPITAL?

There are some persons who imagine that capital is money, and this is precisely the reason why they deny its productiveness; for, as John Ruskin and others say, dollars are not endowed with the power of reproducing themselves. But it is not true that capital and money are the same thing. Before the discovery of the precious metals, there were capitalists in the world; and I venture to say that at that time, as now, everybody was a capitalist, to a certain extent.

What is capital, then? It is composed of three things :—

1st. Of the materials upon which men operate, when these materials have already a value communicated by human effort, which has bestowed upon them the property of exchangeability—wool, flax, leather, silk, wood, etc.

2d. Instruments which are used for working —tools, machines, ships, carriages, etc.

3d. Provisions which are consumed during labor—victuals, stuffs, houses, etc.

Without these things the labor of man would be unproductive and almost void; yet these very things have required much work, especially at first. This is the reason that so much value has been attached to the possession of them, and also that it is perfectly lawful to exchange and to sell them, to make a profit off them if used, to gain remuneration from them if lent.

Now for my anecdotes.

THE SACK OF CORN?

William, in other respects as poor as Job, and obliged to earn his bread by day-labor, became, nevertheless, by some inheritance, the owner of a fine piece of uncultivated land. He was exceedingly anxious to cultivate it. "Alas!" said he, "to make ditches, to raise fences, to break the soil, to clear away the brambles and stones, to plow it, to sow it, might bring me a living in a year or two; but certainly not to-day, or to-morrow. It is impossible to set about farming it, without previously saving some provisions for my subsistence until the harvest; and I know, by experience, that preparatory labor is indispensable in order to render present labor productive." The good William was not content with making these reflections. He resolved to work by the day, and to save something from his wages to buy a spade and a sack of corn, without which things he must give up his agricultural projects. He acted so well, was so active and steady, that he soon saw himself in possession of the wished-for sack of corn. "I shall have enough to live upon till my field is covered with a rich harvest." Just as he was starting, David came to borrow his accumulation of food of him. "If you will lend me this sack of corn," said David, "you will do me a great service; for I have some very lucrative work in view, which I cannot possibly undertake, for want of provisions to live upon till it is finished." "I was in the same case," answered William; "and if I have now secured bread for several months, it is at the expense of my arms and my stomach. Upon what principle of justice can it be devoted to the carrying out of *your* enterprise instead of *mine?*"

You may well believe that the bargain was a

long one. However, it was finished at length, and on these conditions:—

First—David promised to give back, at the end of the year, a sack of corn of the same quality, and of the same weight, without missing a single grain. "This first clause is perfectly just," said he, "for without it William would *give*, and not *lend*."

Secondly—He further engaged to deliver *one-half bushel of corn for every five bushels originally borrowed, when the loan was returned.* "This clause is no less just than the other," thought he; "for unless William would do me a service without compensation, he would inflict upon himself a privation—he would renounce his cherished enterprise—he would enable me to accomplish mine—he would cause me to enjoy for a year the fruits of his savings, and all this gratuitously. Since he delays the cultivation of his land, since he enables me to prosecute a lucrative employment, it is quite natural that I should let him partake, in a certain proportion, of the profits which I shall gain by the sacrifice he makes of his own profits."

On his side, William, who was something of a scholar, made this calculation:—"Since, by virtue of the first clause, the sack of corn will return to me at the end of a year," he said to himself,

"I shall be able to lend it again; it will return to me at the end of the second year; I may lend it again, and so on, to all eternity. However, I cannot deny that it will have been eaten long ago. It is singular that I should be perpetually the owner of a sack of corn, although the one I have lent has been consumed forever. But this is explained thus:—It will be consumed in the service of David. It will put it into the power of David to produce a greater value; and consequently, David will be able to restore me a sack of corn, or the value of it, without having suffered the slightest injury; but, on the contrary, having gained from the use of it. And as regards myself, this value ought to be my property, as long as I do not consume it myself. If I had used it to clear my land, I should have received it again in the form of a fine harvest. Instead of that, I lend it, and shall recover it in the form of repayment.

"From the second clause, I gain another piece of information. At the end of the year I shall be in possession of one bushel of corn for every ten that I may lend. If, then, I were to continue to work by the day, and to save part of my wages, as I have been doing, in the course of time I should be able to lend two sacks of corn; then three; then four; and when I should have gained a sufficient number to enable me to live on these additions of a half a bushel over and above and on account of every ten bushels lent, I shall be at liberty to take a little repose in my old age. But how is this? In this case, shall I not be living at the expense of others? No, certainly, for it has been proved that in lending I perform a service; I make more profitable the labor of my borrowers, and only deduct a trifling part of the excess of production, due to my lendings and savings. It is a marvelous thing that a man may thus realize a leisure which injures no one, and for which he cannot be reproached without injustice."

THE HOUSE.

Again, Thomas had a house. In building it, he had extorted nothing from any one whatever. He obtained it by his own personal labor, or, which is the same thing, by the labor of others justly rewarded. His first care was to make a bargain with an architect, in virtue of which, on condition of the payment of a hundred dollars a year, the latter engaged to keep the house in constant good repair. Thomas was already congratulating himself on the happy days which he hoped to spend in this pleasant home, which our laws declared to be his own exclusive property. But Richard wished to use it also as his residence.

"How can you think of such a thing?" said Thomas to Richard. "It is I who have built it; it has cost me ten years of painful labor, and now you would come in and take it for your enjoyment?" They agreed to refer the matter to judges. They chose no profound economists—there were none such in the country. But they found some just and sensible men; it all comes to the same thing; political economy, justice, good sense, are all the same thing. And here is the decision made by the judges:—If Richard wishes to occupy Thomas's house for a year, he is bound to submit to three conditions. The first is to quit at the end of the year, and to restore the house in good repair, saving the inevitable decay resulting from mere duration. The second, to refund to Thomas the one hundred dollars which Thomas pays annually-to the architect to repair the injuries of time; for these injuries taking place whilst the house is in the service of Richard, it is perfectly just that he should bear the expense. The third, that he should render to Thomas a service equivalent to that which he receives. And as to what shall constitute this equivalence of services, this must be left for Thomas and Richard to mutually agree upon.

THE PLANE.

One further illustration to the same effect. A very long time ago there lived, in a poor village, a joiner, who was a philosopher, as all my heroes are in their way. James worked from morning till night with his two strong arms, but his brain was not idle for all that. He was fond of reviewing his actions, their causes, and their effects. He sometimes said to himself, " With my hatchet, my saw, and my hammer, I can make only coarse furniture, and can only get the pay for such. If I only had a *plane*, I should please my customers more, and they would pay me more. But this is all right; I can only expect services proportioned to those which I render myself. Yes! I am resolved, I will make myself a *plane*."

However, just as he was setting to work, James reflected further :—" I work for my customers 300 days in the year. If I give ten to making my plane, supposing it lasts me a year, only 290 days will remain for me to make my furniture. Now, in order that I be not the loser in this matter, I must gain henceforth, with the help of the plane, as much in 290 days as I now do in 300. I must even gain more; for unless I do so, it would not be worth my while to venture upon any innovations." James began to calculate. He satisfied himself that he should sell his finished furniture at a price which would amply compensate him for the ten days devoted to the plane; and when no doubt remained in his mind on this point, he set to work. I beg the reader to remark, that the power which exists in the tool to increase the productiveness of labor, is the basis for the successful solution of the experiment which James the joiner proposed to make.

At the end of ten days, James had in his possession an admirable plane, which he valued all the more for having made it himself. He danced for joy,—for, like the girl with her basket of eggs, he reckoned in anticipation all the profits which he expected to derive from the ingenious instrument; but, more fortunate than she, he was not reduced to the necessity of saying good-by, when the eggs were smashed, to the expected calf, cow, pig, as well as the eggs, together. He was building his fine castles in the air, when he was interrupted by his acquaintance William, a joiner in the neighboring village. William having admired the plane, was struck with the advantages which might be gained from it. He said to James:—

W. You must do me a service.

J. What service?

W. Lend me the plane for a year.

As might be expected, James at this proposal did not fail to cry out, "How can you think of such a thing, William? But if I do you this service, what will you do for me in return?"

W. Nothing. Don't you know that John Ruskin says a loan ought to be gratuitous? Don't you know that Prudhon and other notable writers and friends of the laboring classes assert that capital is naturally unproductive? Don't you known that all the new school of liberal advanced writers say we ought to have perfect fraternity among men? If you only do me a service for the sake of receiving one from me in return, what merit would you have?

J. William, my friend, fraternity does not mean that all the sacrifices are to be on one side; if so, I do not see why they should not be on yours. Whether a loan should be gratuitous I don't know; but I do know that if I were to lend you my plane for a year it would be giving it you. To tell you the truth, that was not what I made it for.

W. Well, we will say nothing about the modern maxims discovered by the friends of the working classes. I ask you to do me a service; what service do you ask me in return?

J. First, then, in a year the plane will be used up, it will be good for nothing. It is only just that you should let me have another exactly like it; or that you should give me money enough to get it repaired; or that you should supply me the ten days which I must devote to replacing it.

W. This is perfectly just. I submit to these conditions. I engage to return it, or to let you have one like it, or the value of the same. I think you must be satisfied with this, and can require nothing further.

J. I think otherwise. I made the plane for myself, and not for you. I expected to gain some advantage from it, by my work being better finished and better paid; by improving my condition. What reason is there that I should make the plane, and you should gain the profit? I might as well ask you to give me your saw and hatchet! What a confusion! Is it not natural that each should keep what he has made with his own hands, as well as his hands themselves? To use without recompense the hands of another, I call slavery; to use without recompense the plane of another, can this be called fraternity?

W. But, then, I have agreed to return it to you at the end of a year, as well polished and as sharp as it is now.

J. We have nothing to do with next year; we are speaking of this year. I have made the plane for the sake of improving my work and condition;

if you merely return it to me in a year, it is you who will gain the profit of it during the whole of that time. I am not bound to do you such a service without receiving anything from you in return; therefore, if you wish for my plane, independently of the entire restoration already bargained for, you must do me a service which we will now discuss; you must grant me remuneration.

And this was what the two finally agreed upon:—William granted a remuneration calculated in such a way that, at the end of the year, James received his plane quite new, and in addition a new plank, as a compensation for the advantages of which he had deprived himself in lending the plane to his friend.

It was impossible for any one acquainted with the transaction to discover the slightest trace in it of oppression or injustice.

The singular part of it is, that, at the end of the year, the plane came into James's possession, and he lent it again; recovered it, and lent it a third and fourth time. It has passed into the hands of his son, who still lends it. Poor plane! how many times has it changed, sometimes its blade, sometimes its handle. It is no longer the same plane, but it has always the same value, at least for James's posterity. Workmen; let us examine into these little stories.

I maintain, first of all, that the *sack of corn* and the *plane* are here the type, the model, a faithful representation, the symbol of all capital; as the half bushel of corn and the plank are the type, the model, the representation, the symbol of all interest. This granted, the following are, it seems to me, a series of consequences, the justice of which it is impossible to dispute.

1st. If the yielding of a plank by the borrower to the lender is a natural, equitable, lawful remuneration, the just price of a real service, we may conclude that, as a general rule, it is in the nature of capital when loaned or used to produce interest. When this capital, as in the foregoing examples, takes the form of an *instrument of labor*, it is clear enough that it ought to bring an advantage to its possessor, to him who has devoted to it his time, his brains, and his strength. Otherwise, why should he have made it? No necessity of life can be immediately satisfied with instruments of labor; no one eats planes or drinks saws, except, indeed, he be a conjuror. If a man determines to spend his time in the production of such things, he must have been led to it by the consideration of the increased power which these instruments give to him; of the time which they save him; of the perfection and rapidity which they give to his labor; in a word, of the advantages which they procure for him. Now, these advantages, which have been obtained by labor, by the sacrifice of time which might have been used for other purposes, are we bound, as soon as they are ready to be enjoyed, to confer gratuitously upon another? Would it be an advance in social order if the law decided thus, and citizens should pay officials for causing such a law to be executed by force? I venture to say that there is not one amongst you who would support it. It would be to legalize, to organize, to systematize injustice itself, for it would be proclaiming that there are men born to render, and others born to receive, gratuitous services. Grant, then, that interest is just, natural, and expedient.

2d. A second consequence, not less remarkable than the former, and, if possible, still more conclusive, to which I call your attention, is this:—*Interest is not injurious to the borrower.* I mean to say, the obligation in which the borrower finds himself, to pay a remuneration for use of capital, cannot do any harm to his condition. Observe, in fact, that James and William are perfectly free, as regards the transaction to which the plane gave occasion. The transaction cannot be accomplished without the consent of one as well as of the other. The worst which can happen is, that James may be too exacting; and in this case, William, refusing the loan, remains as he was before. By the fact of his agreeing to borrow, he proves that he considers it an advantage to himself; he proves, that after every calculation, whatever may be the remuneration or interest required of him, he still finds it more profitable to borrow than not to borrow. He only determines to do so because he has compared the inconveniences with the advantages. He has calculated that the day on which he returns the plane, accompanied by the remuneration agreed upon, he will have effected more work, with the same labor, thanks to this tool. A profit will remain to him, otherwise he would not have borrowed. The two services of which we are speaking are exchanged according to the law which governs all exchanges, the law of supply and demand. The claims of James have a natural and impassable limit. This is the point in which the remuneration demanded by him would absorb all the advantage which William might find in making use of a plane. In this case, the borrowing would not take place. William would be bound either to make a plane for himself, or do without one, which would leave him in his original condition. He borrows, because he gains by borrowing. I know very well what will be told me. You will say, William may be deceived, or, perhaps, he may be governed by necessity, and be obliged to submit to a harsh law.

It may be so. As to errors in calculation, they belong to the infirmity of our nature, and to argue from this against the transaction in question, is objecting the possibility of loss in all imaginable transactions, in every human act. Error is an accidental fact, which is incessantly remedied by experience. In short, everybody must guard against it. As far as those hard necessities are concerned, which force persons to borrow under onerous conditions, it is clear that these necessities existed previously to the borrowing. If William is in a situation in which he cannot possibly do without a plane, and must borrow one at any price, does this situation result from James having taken the trouble to make the tool? Does it not exist independently of this circumstance? However harsh, however severe James may be, he will never render the supposed condition of William worse than it is. Morally, it is true, the leader will be to blame if he demands more than is just; but, in an economical point of view, the loan itself can never be considered responsible for previous necessities, which it has not created, and which it relieves to a certain extent.

But this proves something to which I shall return. It is evidently for the interest of William, representing here the borrowers, that there shall be many Jameses and planes, or, in other words, lenders and capitals. It is very evident, that if William can say to James, " Your demands are exorbitant; there is no lack of planes in the world;" he will be in a better situation than if James's plane was the only one he could borrow. Assuredly, there is no maxim more true than this —service for service. But let us not forget that no service has a fixed and absolute value, compared with others. The contracting parties are free. Each carries his requisitions to the farthest possible point, and the most favorable circumstance for these requisitions is the absence of rivalship. Hence it follows that if there is a class of men more interested than any other in the creation, multiplication, and abundance of capitals, it is mainly that of the borrowers. Now, since capitals can only be formed and increased by the stimulus and the prospect of remuneration, let this class understand the injury they are inflicting on themselves when they deny the lawlessness of interest, when they proclaim that credit should be gratuitous, when they declaim against the pretended tyranny of capital, when they discourage saving, thus forcing capital to become scarce, and consequently interest to rise.

3d. The anecdote I have just related enables

you to explain this apparently singular phenomenon, which is termed the duration or perpetuity of interest. Since, in lending his plane, James has been able, very lawfully, to make it a condition that it should be returned to him, at the end of a year, in the same state in which it was when he lent it, is it not evident that he may, at the expiration of the term, lend it again on the same conditions? If he resolves upon the latter plan, the plane will return to him at the end of every year, and that without end. James will then be in a condition to lend without end; that is, he may derive from it a perpetual interest. It will be said, that the plane will be worn out. That is true; but it will be worn out by the hand and for the profit of the borrower. The latter has taken this gradual wear into account, and taken upon himself, as he ought, the consequences. He has reckoned that he shall derive from this tool an advantage which will allow him to restore it in its original condition, after having realized a profit from it. As long as James does not use this capital himself, or for his own advantage—as long as he renounces the advantages which allow it to be restored to its original condition—he will have an incontestable right to have it restored, and that independently of interest.

Observe, besides, that if, as I believe I have

shown, James, far from doing any harm to William, has done him a *service* in lending him his plane for a year; for the same reason, he will do no harm to a second, a third, a fourth borrower, in the subsequent periods. Hence you may understand that the interest of a capital is as natural, as lawful, as useful, in the thousandth year, as in the first. We may go still further. It may happen that James lends more than a single plane. It is possible, that by means of working, of saving, of privations, of order, of activity, he may come to be able to lend a multitude of planes and saws; that is to say, to do a multitude of services. I insist upon this point,—that if the first loan has been a social good, it will be the same with all the others; for they are all similar, and based upon the same principle. It may happen, then, that the amount of all the remunerations received by our honest operative, in exchange for services rendered by him, may suffice to maintain him. In this case, there will be a man in the world who has a right to live without working. I do not say that he would be doing right to give himself up to idleness—but I say, that he has a right to do so; and if he does so, it will be at nobody's expense, but quite the contrary. If society at all understands the nature of things, it will acknowledge that this man subsists on services which he receives certainly (as we all do), but which he receives lawfully in exchange for other services, which he himself has rendered, that he continues to render, and which are real services, inasmuch as they are freely and voluntarily accepted.

And here we have a glimpse of one of the finest harmonies in the social word. I allude to *leisure:* not that leisure that the warlike and tyrannical classes arrange for themselves by the plunder of the workers, but that leisure which is the lawful and innocent fruit of past activity and economy. In expressing myself thus, I know that I shall shock many received ideas. But see! Is not leisure an essential spring in the social machine? Without it the world would never have had a Newton, a Pascal, a Fênelon; mankind would have been ignorant of all arts, sciences, and of those wonderful inventions prepared originally by investigations of mere curiosity; thought would have been inert—man would have made no progress.* On the other hand, if leisure could only be

---

* "Of all the results which are produced among a people by their climate, food, and soil, the accumulation of wealth (capital) is the earliest, and in many respects the most important. For although the progress of knowledge eventually accelerates the increase of wealth, it is nevertheless certain that, in the first formation of society, the wealth must accumulate before the knowledge can begin. As long as every man is engaged in collecting the materials necessary

explained by plunder and oppression—if it were a benefit which could only be enjoyed unjustly, and at the expense of others, there would be no middle path between these two evils; either mankind would be reduced to the necessity of stagnating in a vegetable and stationary life, in eternal ignorance, from the absence of wheels to its machine—or else it would have to acquire these wheels at the price of inevitable injustice, and would necessarily present the sad spectacle, in one form or other, of the ancient classification of human beings into masters and slaves. I defy any one to show me, in this case, any other alternative. We should be compelled to contemplate the Divine plan which governs society, with the regret of thinking that it presents a deplorable chasm. The stimulus of progress would be forgotten, or, which is worse, this stimulus would be no other than injustice itself. But no! God has not left such a chasm in His work of love. We must take care not to disregard His wisdom and power; for those whose imperfect meditations

---

for his own subsistence, there will be neither leisure nor taste for higher pursuits. But if the produce is greater than consumption, an overplus arises, by means of which men can use what they did not produce, and are thus enabled to devote themselves to subjects for which at an earlier period the pressure of their daily wants would have left them no time."—*Buckle's History of Civilization.*

cannot explain the lawfulness of leisure, are very much like the astronomer who said, at a certain point in the heavens there ought to exist a planet which will be at last discovered, for without it the celestial world is not harmony, but discord.

Therefore, I say that, if well understood, the history of my humble plane, although very modest, is sufficient to raise us to the contemplation of one of the most consoling, but least understood of the social harmonies.

It is not true that we must choose between the denial or the unlawfulness of leisure; thanks to rent and its natural duration, leisure may arise from labor and saving. It is a pleasing prospect, which every one may have in view; a noble recompense, to which each may aspire. It makes its appearance in the world; it distributes itself proportionably to the exercise of certain virtues; it opens all the avenues to intelligence; it ennobles, it raises the morals; it spiritualizes the soul of humanity, not only without laying any weight on those of our brethren whose lot in life makes severe labor necessary, but it relieves them gradually from the heaviest and most repugnant part of this labor. It is enough that capitals should be formed, accumulated, multiplied; should be lent on conditions less and less burdensome; that they should descend, penetrate into every social circle, and that by an admirable progression, after having liberated the lenders from onerous toil, they should bring a similar liberation to the borrowers themselves. For that end, the laws and customs ought all to be favorable to economy, the source of capital. It is enough to say, that the first of all these conditions is, not to alarm, to attack, to deny that which is the stimulus of saving and the reason of its existence—interest.

As long as we see nothing passing from hand to hand, in the operations of loan, but *provisions, materials, instruments*, things indispensable to the productiveness of labor itself, the ideas thus far exhibited will not find many opponents. Who knows, even, that I may not be reproached for having made a great effort to burst what may be said to be an open door? But as soon as money makes its appearance as the subject of the transaction (and it is this which appears almost always), immediately a crowd of objections are raised. Money, it will be said, will not reproduce itself, like your *sack of corn;* it does not assist labor, like your *plane;* it does not afford an immediate satisfaction, like your *house*. It is incapable, by its nature, of producing interest, of multiplying itself, and the remuneration it demands is a positive extortion.

Who cannot see the sophistry of this? Who

does not see that money is only an instrumentality which men use to represent other *values*, or real objects of usefulness, for the sole object of facilitating their exchanges of commodities or services? In the midst of social complications, the man who is in a condition to lend scarcely ever has the exact thing which the borrower wants. James, it is true, has a plane; but, perhaps, William wants a saw. They cannot negotiate; the transaction favorable to both cannot take place, and then what happens? It happens that James first exchanges his plane for money; he lends the money to William, and William exchanges the money for a saw. The transaction is no longer a simple one; it is resolved into two transactions, as I explained above in speaking of exchange. But, for all that, it has not changed its nature; it still contains all the elements of a direct loan. James has parted with a tool which was useful to him; William has at the same time received an instrument which facilitates his work and increases his profits; there is still a service rendered by the lender, which entitles him to receive an equivalent service from the borrower; and this just balance is not the less established by free mutual bargaining. The obvious natural obligation to restore at the end of the term the *entire value* of what was borrowed still constitutes the principle of the rightfulness of interest.

At the end of a year, says M. Thoré, will you find an additional dollar in a bag of a hundred dollars?

No, certainly if the borrower puts the bag of one hundred dollars on the shelf. In such a case, neither the plane nor the sack of corn would reproduce themselves. But it is not for the sake of leaving the money in the bag, nor the plane on the shelf, that they are borrowed. The plane is borrowed to be used, or the money to procure a plane. And if it is clearly proved that this tool enables the borrower to obtain profits which he could not have made without it; if it is proved that the lender has given up the opportunity of creating for himself this excess of profits, we may understand how the stipulation of a part of this excess of profits in favor of the lender, is equitable and lawful.

Ignorance of the true part which money plays in human transactions, is the source of the most fatal errors. From what we may infer from the writings of M. Proudhon, that which has led him to think that gratuitous credit was a logical and definite consequence of social progress, is the observation of the phenomenon that interest seems to decrease almost in direct proportion to the progress of civilization. In barbarous times it is, in fact, cent. per cent., and more. Then it descends to eighty, sixty, fifty, forty, twenty, ten, eight, five, four, and three per cent. In Holland, it has even been as low as two per cent. Hence it is concluded, that "in proportion as society comes to perfection, the rate of interest will diminish and finally run down to zero, or nothing, by the time civilization is complete. In other words, that which characterizes social perfection is the gratuitousness of credit. When, therefore, we shall have abolished interest, we shall have reached the last step of progress." This is mere sophistry, and as such false arguing may contribute to render popular the unjust, dangerous, and destructive dogma that credit should be gratuitous, by representing it as coincident with social perfection, with the reader's permission I will examine in a few words this new view of the question.

WHAT REGULATES INTEREST?

What is *interest?* It is the service rendered, after a free bargain, by the borrower to the lender, in remuneration for the service he has received by or from the loan. By what law is the rate of these remunerative services established? By the general law which regulates the equivalent of all services; that is, by the law of supply and demand.

The more easily a thing is procured, the smaller

is the service rendered by yielding it or lending it. The man who gives me a glass of water among the springs of the mountains does not render me so great a service as he who allows me one in the desert of Sahara. If there are many planes, sacks of corn, or houses, in a country, the use of them is obtained, other things being equal, on more favourable conditions than if they were few, for the simple reason that the lender renders in this case a smaller *relative service*.

It is not surprising, therefore, that the more abundant capital is, the lower is the interest.

Is this saying that it will ever reach zero? No; because, I repeat it, the principle of a remuneration is in the loan. To say that interest will be annihilated, is to say that there will never be any motive for saving, for denying ourselves, in order to form new capitals, nor even to preserve the old ones. In this case, the waste would immediately create a void, and interest would directly reappear.

In that, the nature of the services of which we are speaking does not differ from any other. Thanks to industrial progress, a pair of stockings, which used to be worth six shillings, has successively been worth only four, three, and two. No one can say to what point this value will descend; but we can affirm that it will never reach zero, unless the stockings finish by producing themselves spontaneously. Why? Because the principle of remuneration is in labor; because he who works for another renders a service, and ought to receive a service. If no one paid for stockings they would cease to be made; and, with the scarcity, the price would not fail to reappear.

The sophism which I am now combating has its root in the infinite divisibility which belongs to *value*, as it does to matter.

It may appear at first paradoxical, but it is well known to all mathematicians, that, through all eternity, fractions may be taken from a weight without the weight ever being annihilated. It is sufficient that each successive fraction be less than the preceding one, in a determined and regular proportion.

There are countries where people apply themselves to increasing the size of horses, or diminishing in sheep the size of the head. It is impossible to say precisely to what point they will arrive in this. No one can say that he has seen the largest horse or the smallest sheep's head that will ever appear in the world. But he may safely say that the size of horses will never attain to infinity, nor the heads of sheep be reduced to nothing.

In the same way, no one can say to what point

the price of stockings nor the interest of capital will come down; but we may safely affirm, when we know the nature of things, that neither the one nor the other will ever arrive at zero, for labor and capital can no more live without recompense than a sheep without a head.

The arguments of Mr. Proudhon reduce themselves, then, to this:—Since the most skillful agriculturists are those who have reduced the heads of sheep to the smallest size, we shall have arrived at the highest agricultural perfection when sheep have no longer any heads. Therefore, in order to realize the perfection, let us behead them.

I have now done with this wearisome discussion. Why is it that the breath of false doctrine has made it needful to examine into the innate nature of interest? I must not leave off without remarking upon a beautiful moral which may be drawn from this law:—"The reduction in the rate of interest is proportional to the abundance of capital." This law being granted, if there is a class of men to whom it is more important than to any other that stocks of capital should accumulate, multiply, abound, and superabound, it is certainly the class which borrows capital directly or indirectly; it is those men who operate upon *materials*, who gain assistance by *instruments*, who live upon accumulations produced and saved by other men.

Imagine, in a vast and fertile country, a population of a thousand inhabitants, destitute of all capital as thus defined. It will assuredly perish by the pangs of hunger. Let us suppose a case hardly less cruel. Let us suppose that ten of these savages (for persons without capital are savages) are provided with instruments and provisions sufficient to work and to live themselves until harvest time, as well as to remunerate the services of eighty laborers. The inevitable result will be the death of nine hundred human beings. It is clear, then, that since 990 men, urged by want, will crowd upon the supports which would only maintain a hundred, the ten capitalists will be masters of the market. They will obtain labor on the hardest conditions, for they will put it up to auction or the highest bidder. And observe this,— if these capitalists entertain such pious sentiments as would induce them to impose personal privations on themselves, in order to diminish the sufferings of some of their brethren, this generosity, which attaches to morality, will be as noble in its principle as useful in its effects. But, if duped by that false philosophy which persons wish so inconsiderately to mingle with economic laws, they take to remunerating labor in excess of what it is worth, and in excess of what they are able to pay, far from doing good, they will do harm. They will give double wages, it may be. But then, forty-five men will be better provided for, whilst forty-five others from the diminution in the supply of capital, will augment the number of those who are sinking into the grave. Upon this supposition, it is not the deprivation of wages which primarily works the mischief, but the scarcity of capital. Low wages are not the cause, but the effect of the evil. I may add, that they are to a certain extent the remedy. It acts in this way: it distributes the burden of suffering as much as it can, and saves as many lives as a limited quantity of available sustenance permits.

Suppose now, that instead of ten capitalists, there should be a hundred, two hundred, five hundred—is it not evident that the condition of the whole population, and, above all, that of the mass of the people will be more and more improved? Is it not evident that, apart from every consideration of generosity, they would obtain more work and better pay for it?—that they themselves will be in a better condition to accumulate capital, without being able to fix the limits to this ever-increasing facility of realizing equality and well-being? Would it not be madness in them to admit and act upon the truth of such doctrines as Proudhon and John Ruskin teach, and to act in a way which would reduce the source of wages, and paralyze the activity and stimulus of saving? Let them learn this lesson, then. Accumulations of capital are good for those who possess them: who denies it? But they are also useful to those who have not yet been able to form them; and it is important to those who have them not that others should have them.

Yes, if the laboring classes knew their true interests, they would seek to know with the greatest earnestness what circumstances are, and what are not favorable to saving, in order to encourage the former and to discourage the latter. They would sympathize with every measure which tends to the rapid accumulation of capital. They would be enthusiastic promoters of peace, liberty, order, security, the union of classes and peoples, economy, moderation in public expenses, simplicity in the machinery of government; for it is under the sway of all these circumstances that saving does its work, brings plenty within the reach of the masses, invites those persons to become the owners of capital who were formerly under the necessity of borrowing upon hard conditions. They would repel with energy the warlike spirit, which diverts from its true course so large a part of human labor; the monopolizing spirit, which deranges the equitable distribution of riches, in the way by which liberty alone can realize it; the multitude of public services which attack our purses only to check our liberty; and, in short, those subversive, hateful, thoughtless doctrines, which alarm capital, prevent its formation, oblige it to flee, and finally to raise its price, to the especial disadvantage of the workers, who bring it into existence.

Take for example the revolution which overthrew the government of France, and disturbed society in February, 1848, is it not a hard lesson? Is it not evident that the insecurity it has thrown into the world of business on the one hand; and, on the other, the advancement of the fatal theories to which I have alluded, and which, from the clubs, have almost penetrated into the regions of the legislature, have everywhere raised the rate of interest? Is it not evident that from that time the laboring classes of France have found greater difficulty in procuring those materials, instruments, and provisions, without which labor is impossible? Is it not that which has caused stagnation of business; and does not paralysis of industry in turn lower wages? Thus there is a deficiency of labor to those who need to labor, from the same cause which loads the objects they consume with an increase of price, in consequence of the rise of interest. High interest and low wages, signify in other words that the same article preserves its price, but that the remuneration of the capitalist has invaded, without profiting himself, that of the workman.

A friend of mine, commissioned to make inquiry into Parisian industry, has assured me that the manufacturers have revealed to him a very striking fact, which proves, better than any reasoning can, how much insecurity and uncertainty injure the formation of capital. It was remarked that during the most distressing period of this revolution the popular expenses of expenditures for personal gratification did not diminish. The small theatres, the public-houses, and tobacco depôts, were as much frequented as in prosperous times. On inquiry, the operatives themselves explained this phenomenon as follows: —" What is the use of economizing? Who knows what will happen to us? Who knows that interest will not be abolished? Who knows but that the State will become a universal and gratuitous lender, and that it will annihilate all the fruits which we might expect from our savings?" Well! I say, that if such ideas could prevail during two single years, it would be enough to turn our beautiful France into a Turkey—misery would become general and endemic, and, most assuredly, the poor would be the first upon whom it would fall.

Laboring men! they talk to you a great deal upon the *artificial* organization of labor;—do you know why they do so? Because they are ignorant of the laws of its *natural* organization; that is, of the wonderful organization which results from liberty. You are told that liberty gives rise to what is called the radical antagonism of classes; that it creates, and makes to clash, two opposite interests—that of the capitalists and that of the laborers. But we ought to begin by proving that the antagonism exists by a law of nature; and afterwards it would remain to be shown how far the arrangements for restriction are superior to those of liberty, for between liberty and restriction I see no middle path. Again, it would remain to be proved that restriction would always operate to your advantage, and to the prejudice of the rich. But, no; this radical antagonism, this natural opposition of interests, does not exist. It is only an evil dream of perverted and intoxicated imaginations. No; a plan so defective has not proceeded from the Divine Mind. To affirm it, we must begin by denying the existence of God. And see how, by means of social laws, and because men exchange amongst themselves their labors and their productions, a harmonious tie attaches the different classes of society one to the other! There are the landowners; what is their interest? That the soil be fertile, and the sun beneficent: and what is the result? That wheat abounds, that it falls in price, and the advantage turns to the profit of those who have had no patrimony. There are the manufacturers—what is their constant thought? To perfect their labor, to increase the power of their machines, to procure for themselves, upon the best terms, the raw material. And to what does all this tend? To the abundance and the low price of produce; that is, all the efforts of the manufacturers, and without their suspecting it, result in a profit to the public consumer, of which each of you is one. It is the same with every profession. Now, the capitalists are not exempt from this law. They are very busy making schemes, economizing, and turning them to their advantage. This is all very well; but the more they succeed, the more do they promote the abundance of capital, and, as a necessary consequence, the reduction of interest. Now, who is it that profits by the reduction of interest? Is it not the borrower first, and finally, the consumers of the things which the capital contributes to produce?

It is therefore certain that the final result of

the efforts of each class is the common good of all.

You are told that capital tyrannizes over labor. I do not deny that each one endeavors to draw the greatest possible advantage from his situation; but, in this sense, he realizes only that which is possible. Now, it is never more possible for capitalists to tyrannize over labor, than when capital is scarce; for then it is they who make the law —it is they who regulate the rate of sale. Never is this tyranny more impossible to them, than when capital and capitalists are abundant; for, in that case, it is labor which has the command. [Where there is one to sell and two to buy, the seller fixes the price; where there are two to sell and one to buy, the buyer always has the advantage.—*Editor.*]

Away, then, with the jealousies of classes, ill-will, unfounded hatreds, unjust suspicions. These depraved passions injure those who nourish them in their heart. This is no declamatory morality; it is a chain of causes and effects, which is capable of being rigorously, mathematically demonstrated. It is not the less sublime in that it satisfies the intellect as well as the feelings.

I shall sum up this whole dissertation with these words:—Workmen, laborers, destitute and suffering classes, will you improve your condition? You will not succeed by strife, insurrection, hatred, and error. But there are three things which always result in benefit and blessing to every community and to every individual which help to compose it;—and these things are—peace, liberty, and security.

The foregoing essay was written by M. Bastiat, in France, for the instruction of his countrymen, shortly after the revolution of 1848, when the opinions of Proudhon and other Socialist leaders seemed to be acquiring a strong hold among the laboring classes of his country. Proudhon, and most of his Socialist friends have passed away, but their ideas nevertheless continue to find favor with not a few people, even in the United States. It may, therefore, be of interest to the American reader, to supplement this essay of M. Bastiat, with the following results of some investigations relative to accumulation and distribution of wealth in the United States, which were presented to the American Social Science Association, at their annual meeting in Detroit, Michigan, in 1875:

"It would seem clear, that all ideas about the compulsory distribution of wealth or capital, and about diminishing the incentives for the accumulation of capital, are wholly antagonistic in the first place, to the idea of personal freedom, unless we mean to restrict the meaning of freedom simply to the possession and control of one's own person irrespective of property, which would involve little more than the right to free locomotion; and, second, that they tend to impair the growth of, if not wholly to destroy, civilization itself. For if liberty is not afforded to all, rich and poor, high and low, to keep, and to use in whatever way they may see fit, that which they lawfully acquire, subject only to the necessary social restraint of working no positive ill to one's neighbor,—then the desire to acquire and accumulate property will be taken away; and capital, meaning thereby not merely money, which constitutes but a very small part of the capital of any community, but all those things which are the accumulated results of labor, foresight, and economy,—the machinery by which abundance is increased, toil lightened, and comfort gained,—will, instead of increasing, rapidly diminish.

"And, in order to comprehend the full meaning of this statement, attention is asked to the following illustration of the extreme slowness with which that which we call capital accumulates, even under the most favorable circumstances.

"By the census of 1870, the aggregate wealth of the United States, making all due allowances for duplication in valuation, was probably not in excess of *twenty-five thousand millions*. But vast as the sum is, and difficult as it certainly is for the mind to form any adequate conception of it in the aggregate, it is nevertheless most interesting to inquire what it is, that measured by human effort, it represents. And the answer is, that it represents, *first*, a value, supposing the whole sum to be apportioned equally among an assumed population of forty millions, of about six hundred and twenty dollars to each individual,—not a large amount, if one was to depend on its interest at six per cent. as a means of support; and, *second*, it represents the surplus result of all the labor, skill, and thought exerted, and all the capital earned and saved, or brought into the country, for the last two hundred and fifty years, or ever since the country became practically the abode of civilized men.

"But, with capital, or the instrumentalities for creating abundance, increasing thus slowly, it certainly stands to reason that we needs be exceedingly careful, lest, by doing anything to impair its security, we impair also its rate of increase; and we accordingly find, as we should naturally expect from the comparatively high education of our people, that the idea of any direct interference with the rights of property meets with but little favor upon this side of the Atlantic. But at the same time we cannot deny that many of the most intelligent of the men and women interested in the various labor-reform movements in this country, taking as the basis of their reasoning the large nominal aggregate of the national wealth, and the large advance which has recently been made in the power of production, and considering them in the abstract, irrespective of time or distribution, have nevertheless adopted the idea,—vague and shadowy though it may be,— that the amount of the present annual product of labor and capital is sufficient for all; and that all it is necessary to do to insure comfort and abundance to the masses, is for the State somehow to intervene,—either by fixing the hours of labor, or the rates of compensation for service, or the use of capital,—and compel its more equitable distribution.

"Now, that a more equitable distribution of the results of production is desirable, and that such a distribution does not at present take place to the extent that it might without impairing the exercise of individual freedom, must be admitted; but, before undertaking to make laws on the subject, is it not of importance to first find out how much we have really got to divide?

"Let us see.

"Stated in money, the maximum value of the annual product of the United States is not in excess of $5,000,000,000 (probably less); of which the value of the annual product of all our agriculture,—our cotton and our corn, our beef and our pork, our hay, our wheat, and all our other fruits,—is returned by the last census with undoubted approximative accuracy, at less than one-half that sum; or in round numbers at $2,400,000,000.

"But while this sum of estimated yearly income, like the figures which report the aggregate of our national wealth, is so vast as to be almost beyond the power of mental conception, there is yet one thing about it which is certain, and can be readily comprehended; and that is, that of this whole product, whether we measure it in money or in any other way, fully nine-tenths, and probably a larger proportion, must be immediately consumed, in order that we may simply live, and make good the loss and waste of capital previously accumulated; leaving not more than *one-tenth* to be applied in the form of accumulation for effecting a future increased production and development.

"Or to state the case differently, and at the same time illustrate how small, even under the most favorable circumstances, can be the annual surplus of production over consumption, it is only necessary to compare the largest estimate of the value of our annual product, with our largest estimate of the aggregate national wealth, to see, that practically, after two hundred and fifty years of toiling and saving, we have only managed as a nation to get about three and a half years ahead, in the way of subsistence; and that now if, as a whole people, we should stop working and producing, and repairing waste and deterioration, and devote ourselves exclusively to amusement and idleness, living on the accumulation of our former labors or the labor of our fathers, four years would be more than sufficient to starve three-fourths of us out of existence, and reduce the other one-fourth to the condition of semi-barbarism; a result, on the whole, which it is well to think of in connection with the promulgation of certain new theories, that the best way of increasing abundance, and promoting comfort and happiness, is by decreasing the aggregate and opportunities of production.

"In fact, there are few things more transitory and perishable than that which we call wealth; and, as specifically embodied in the ordinary forms we see about us, its duration is not, on the average, in excess of the life of a generation.

"The railroad system of the country is estimated to have cost more than two thousand millions of dollars; but if left to itself, without renewals or repairs, its value as property in ten years would entirely vanish; and so also with our ships, our machinery, our tools and implements, and even our land when cultivated without renovation. For it is to be remembered, that those same forces of nature which we have mastered, and made subservient for the work of production, are also our greatest natural enemies, and if left to themselves will tear down and destroy much more rapidly than under guidance they will aggregate and build up. A single night was sufficient in Chicago to utterly destroy what was equivalent to one quarter of the whole surplus product which during the preceding year the nation had accumulated; and of all the material wealth of the great and rich nations of antiquity, —of Egyptian, Assyrian, Tyrian, and Roman civilization,—nothing whatever has come down to us, except, singularly enough, those things which, like their tombs and public monuments, never were possessed of a money valuation.

"But the inferences which we are warranted in drawing from these facts and figures are by no means exhausted. Supposing the value of our annual product—five thousand millions—to be equally divided among our present population of forty millions: then the average income of each individual would be one hundred and twenty-five dollars per annum; out of which food, clothing, fuel, shelter, education, traveling expenses, and means of enjoyment, are to be provided, all taxes paid, all waste, loss, and depreciation made good, and any surplus available as new capital added to former accumulations.

"Now, if at first thought this deduction of the average individual income of our people seems small, it should be remembered that it is based on an estimate of annual national product greater both in the aggregate, and in proportion to numbers, than is enjoyed by any other nation, our compeers in wealth and civilization; and further, that this one hundred and twenty-five dollars is not the sum which all actually receive as income, but the average sum which each would receive, were the whole annual product divided equally. But as a practical matter we know that the annual product is not divided equally; and, furthermore, that, as long as men are born with different natural capacities, it never will be so divided. Some will receive, and do receive, as their share of the annual product, the annual average we have stated, multiplied by hundreds or even thousands; which of course necessitates that very many others shall receive proportionally less. And how much less, is indicated by recent investigations which show, that for the whole country the average earnings of laborers and unskilled workmen is not in excess of four hundred dollars per annum,—the maximum amount being received in New England, and the minimum in the Southern, or former slaveholding States; which sum, assuming that the families of all these men consist of four (the census of 1875 says five), two adults and two children, would give one hundred dollars as the average amount which each individual of the class referred to produces, and also the amount to which each such individual must be restricted in consumption; for it is clear, that no man can consume more than he or his capital produces, unless he can in some way obtain the product of some other man's labor without giving him an equivalent for it.

"We are thus led to the conclusion, that notwithstanding the wonderful extent to which we have been enabled to use and control the forces of nature for the purpose of increasing the power of production, the time has not yet come, when society in the United States can command such a degree of absolute abundance as to justify and warrant any class or individual, rich or poor, and least of all those who depend upon the product of each day's labor to meet each day's needs, in doing anything which can in any way tend to diminish abundance; and furthermore, that the agency of law, even if invoked to the fullest extent in compelling distribution, must be exceedingly limited in its operations.

"Let the working man of the United States therefore, in every vocation, demand and strive, if he will, for the largest possible share of the joint products of labor and capital; for it is the natural right of every one to seek to obtain the largest price for that which he has to sell. But if in so doing he restricts production, and so diminishes abundance, he does it at his peril; for, by a law far above any legislative control or influence, whatever increases scarcity not only increases the necessity, but diminishes the rewards of labor.

"Street processions, marching after flags and patriotic mottoes, even if held every day in the week, will never change the conditions which govern production and compensation. 'Idleness produces nothing but weeds and rust; and such products are not marketable anywhere, though society often pays for them most dearly.'"

—Editor.

THAT WHICH IS SEEN,

AND

THAT WHICH IS NOT SEEN.

In the department of economy, an act, a habit, an institution, a law, gives birth not only to an effect, but to a series of effects. Of these effects, the first only is immediate; it manifests itself simultaneously with its cause—*it is seen*. The others unfold in succession—*they are not seen:* it is well for us if they are *foreseen*. Between a good and a bad economist this constitutes the whole difference—the one takes account of the *visible* effect; the other takes account both of the effects which are *seen* and also of those which it is necessary to *foresee*. Now this difference is enormous, for it sometimes happens that when the immediate consequence is favorable, the ultimate consequences are unfavorable, *and the converse*. Hence it follows that the bad economist pursues a small present good, which may be followed by a great evil to come, while the wise economist labors for a great good to come, at the risk of a small present evil.

In fact, it is the same in the science of health, arts, and in that of morals. If often happens that the sweeter the first fruit of a habit is, the more bitter the consequences. Take, for example, debauchery, idleness, prodigality. When, therefore, a man, absorbed in the effect which *is seen*, has not yet learned to discern those which are not seen, he gives way to injurious habits, not only by inclination but by deliberation.

This explains, in a great degree, the grievous condition of mankind. Ignorance surrounds its cradle: then its actions are determined by their first consequences, the only ones which, in its first stage, it can see. It is only in the long run that it learns to take account of the others. It has to learn this lesson from two very different masters —experience and foresight. Experience teaches effectually, but brutally. It makes us acquainted with all the effects of an action, by causing us to feel them; and we cannot fail to finish by knowing that fire burns, if we have burned ourselves. For this rough teacher, I should like, if possible, to substitute a more gentle one. I mean Foresight. For this purpose I propose to examine the consequences of certain economical phenomena, by placing in opposition to each other those *which are seen*, and those *which are not seen*.

I.—THE BROKEN WINDOW.

Have you ever witnessed the anger of the good shopkeeper, James, when his careless son happened to break a pane of glass? If you have been present at such a scene, you will most assuredly bear witness to the fact, that it is the custom of the spectators to offer the unfortunate owner this invariable consolation: "It is an ill wind that blows nobody good. Everybody must live, and what would become of the glaziers if panes of glass were never broken?"

Now, this form of condolence contains an entire theory, which it will be well to show up in this simple case, seeing that it is precisely the same as that which, unhappily, regulates the greater part of our economical institutions.

Suppose it cost a dollar to repair the damage, and you say that the accident brings a dollar to the glazier's trade—that it encourages that trade to the amount of a dollar—I grant it; I have not a word to say against it; you reason justly. The glazier comes, performs his task, receives his dollar, rubs his hands, and, in his heart, blesses the careless child. All this is *that which is seen*.

But if, on the other hand, you come to the conclusion, as is too often the case, that it is a good thing to break windows, that it causes money to circulate, and that the encouragement of industry in general will be the result of it, you will oblige me to call out, "Stop there! your theory is confined to that *which is seen;* it takes no account of that *which is not seen.*"

It is not seen that as our shopkeeper has spent a dollar upon one thing, he cannot spend it again upon some other thing. *It is not seen* that if he had not had a window to replace, he would, perhaps, have replaced his old shoes, or added another book to his library. In short, he would have employed his dollar in some way which this accident has prevented.

Let us take a view of industry in general, as affected by this circumstance. The window being broken, the glazier's trade is encouraged to the amount of a dollar: *this is that which is seen.*

If the window had not been broken, the shoemaker's trade (or some other) would have been encouraged to the amount of a dollar; this is *that which is not seen.*

And if *that which is not seen* is taken into consideration, because it is a negative fact, as well as that which is seen, because it is a positive fact, it will be understood that neither industry *in*

4

general, nor the sum total of *national labor*, is affected, whether windows are broken or not.

Now let us consider James himself. In the former supposition, that of the window being broken, he spends a dollar, and has neither more nor less than he had before—namely, the enjoyment of a window.

In the second, where we suppose the window not to have been broken, he would have spent his dollar in shoes, and would have had at the same time the enjoyment of a pair of shoes and of a window.

Now, as James forms a part of society, we must come to the conclusion, that, taking it altogether, and making an estimate of its enjoyments and its labors, society has lost the value of the broken window.

Whence we arrive at this unexpected conclusion: "Society loses the value of things which are uselessly destroyed;" and we must assent to a maxim which will make the hair of protectionists stand on end—To break, to spoil, to waste, is not to encourage national labor; or, more briefly, "destruction is not profit."

What will you say to this, Mr. H. C. Carey? what will you say, disciples of good Mr. Horace Greeley, who moralized and considered how much American industry would gain by the burning of

Chicago, in October, 1871, from the number of houses it would be necessary to rebuild?*

I am sorry to disturb these ingenious calcula-

---

* As M. Bastiat originally wrote, he introduced at this point of his argument, for illustration, French names and persons not familiar to the American reader; and if the translation had been made literal, the majority of Americans, as they read, would doubtless have said to themselves: "*These names which M. Bastiat uses are purely fictitious; for surely one really and soberly never put forth such ideas, or entered into such estimates.*" To give, therefore, to the argument more of force and reality; to prove that there is no necessity of using fictitious names and characters in its presentation; but that persons of position, intelligence, and great influence do think, talk, and believe as M. Bastiat assumes, not only in France, but also in the United States, the editor has substituted in the text the names of two well-known Americans. And that he has taken no unwarranted liberty in so doing, he submits the following as evidence. Thus, on the 24th of October, 1871, the *New York Tribune*, then controlled by Horace Greeley, in an article in its editorial columns, evidently written by Mr. Greeley, thus reasoned about the great fire which had occurred a few days previous at Chicago:—

"The money to replace what has been burned will not be sent abroad to enrich foreign manufacturers; but thanks to the wise policy of protection, it will stimulate our own manufactures, set our mills to running faster, and give employment to thousands of idle workmen. Thus in a short time our abundant natural resources will restore what has been lost, and in converting the raw material our manufacturing interests will take on a new activity."

All of which is equivalent to saying, "that fire, war, pestitions, as far as their spirit has been introduced into our political economy; but I beg of those who have indulged in them to consider the subject again, from a broader point of view, by taking into the account *that which is not seen,* and placing it alongside of *that which is seen.*

The reader must take care to remember that there are not two persons only, but three concerned in the little scene which I have submitted to his attention. One of them, James, repre-

---

lence, famine, shipwreck, and other calamities, if they give to certain class interests an opportunity to make and sell products at an advance over their current prices in the world's markets, and thereby inflict an unnecessary and large additional tax on the impoverished inhabitants of a distressed city, are not to be regarded wholly in the light of evils and disasters." The inhabitants of Chicago, following their natural instincts, could not, however, see the applicability of Mr. Greeley's reasoning in respect to themselves, for they forthwith petitioned Congress to allow foreign merchandise, useful for rebuilding their stores and houses, to be imported free of duty; and Congress, also disagreeing with Mr. Greeley, acceded to their petition.

Again, Mr. Henry C. Carey, who is one of the foremost advocates of the "Protection Theory," has within recent years said publicly, over and over again, that one of the greatest of human calamities—a prolonged war between Great Britain and the United States—would be the very best possible thing which could happen to promote the industrial independence and development of the latter country.—
Editor.

sents the consumer, reduced, by an act of destruction, to one enjoyment instead of two. Another, under the title of the glazier, shows us the producer, whose trade is encouraged by the accident. The third is the shoemaker (or some other tradesman), whose labor suffers proportionably by the same cause. It is this third person who is always kept in the shade, and who, personating *that which is not seen*, is a necessary element of the problem. It is he who shows us how absurd it is to think we see a profit in an act of destruction. It is he who will soon teach us that it is not less absurd to see a profit in a restriction, which is, after all, nothing else than a partial destruction. Therefore, if you will only go to the root of all the arguments which are adduced in its favor, all you will find will be the paraphrase of this vulgar saying—*What would become of the glazier, if nobody ever broke windows?*

II.—THE DISBANDING OF TROOPS.

It is the same with a people as it is with a man. If it wishes to give itself some gratification, it naturally considers whether it is worth what it costs. To a nation, security is the greatest of advantages. If, in order to obtain it, it is necessary to have an army of a hundred thousand men, I have nothing to say against it. It is an enjoyment bought by a sacrifice of a certain amount of the results of labor, which might be used for other purposes. Let me not be misunderstood upon the extent of my position. A member of Congress proposes to disband a hundred thousand men, for the sake of relieving the tax-payers of an annual tax of fifty millions of dollars.

If we confine ourselves to this answer—" The hundred millions of men, and these hundred millions of money, are indispensable to the national security. It is security purchased at the sacrifice of a certain amount of property; but without this sacrifice the country might be torn by factions or invaded by some foreign power." I have nothing to object to this argument, which may be true or false in fact, but which theoretically contains nothing which militates against political economy. The error begins when the sacrifice itself is said to be an advantage because it profits somebody.

Now I am very much mistaken if, the moment the author of the proposal has taken his seat, some orator will not rise and say—" Disband a hundred thousand men! Do you know what you are saying? What will become of them? Where will they get a living? Don't you know that work is scarce everywhere? That every field is overstocked? Would you turn them out of doors to increase competition and to still further depress the rate of wages? Just now, when it is a hard matter to live at all, it is a pretty business for the State to add an additional hundred thousand persons to the number of the community who must get bread by their own labor. Consider, also, that the army consumes arms, clothing, and a great variety of other products of labor; that it makes business in garrison towns; that it is, in short, an immense blessing to innumerable purveyors. Why, the very bare idea of doing away with all this immense industrial movement is enough to terrify every one who has at heart the development of the business of the country. Such talk always has an effect on all patriotic generous minds, and Congress terminates the discussion by voting the continued maintenance of the hundred thousand soldiers, for reasons drawn from the necessity of the service, and from economical considerations. It is these latter considerations only that I have to consider.

A hundred thousand men, costing the tax-payers fifty millions of money, live and bring to the purveyors as much as that fifty millions can supply. This is *that which is seen.*

But fifty millions taken from the pockets of the tax-payers cease to maintain these same tax-payers and the purveyors, to the extent to which these fifty millions are invested with a purchasing power of the necessities of life. This is *that which is not seen.* Now make your calculations. Cast up, and tell me what profit there is for the masses?

I will tell you where the *loss* lies; and to simplify it, instead of speaking of a hundred thousand men and fifty millions of money, it shall be of one man and five hundred dollars of money.

We will suppose that we are in the village of A. The recruiting sergeants go their round, and take off a man. The United States tax-collectors go their round, and take off five hundred dollars, the results of taxation. The man and the sum of money are taken to form a camp—say at Washington—and the money is appropriated to support the soldier for a year without doing anything. If you now have regard to the interest of the city and population of Washington only, the measure is a very advantageous one; but if you look toward the village of A., you will judge very differently; for, unless you are very blind indeed, you will see that that village has lost a worker, and the five hundred dollars which would remunerate his labor, as well as the activity which the expenditure of that money taken away in the form of taxes would locally produce.

At first sight there would seem to be some compensation. What took place at the village now takes place at Washington, that is all. But the loss is to be estimated in this way:—At the village, a man dug and worked; he was a worker. At Washington, he turns to the right about and to the left about; he is a soldier. The money and the circulation are the same in both cases; but in the one there were three hundred days of productive labor, in the other there are three hundred days of unproductive labor, supposing, of course, that a part of the army is not indispensable to the public safety.

Now, suppose the disbanding to take place. You tell me there will be a surplus of a hundred thousand workers, that competition will be stimulated, and it will reduce the rate of wages. This is what you see.

But what you do not see is this. You do not see that to dismiss a hundred thousand soldiers is not to annihilate or use up the fifty millions of money, but to return it to the tax-payers. You do not see that to throw a hundred thousand workers on the market, is to throw into it, at the same moment, the fifty millions of money needed to pay for their labor: that, consequently, the same act which increases the supply of hands, increases also the demand; from which it follows, that your fear of a reduction of wages is unfounded. You do not see that, before the disbanding as well as after it, there are in the country fifty millions of money corresponding with the hundred thousand men. That the whole difference consists in this: before the disbanding, the country gave the fifty millions to the hundred thousand men for doing nothing; and that after it, it pays them the same sum for working. You do not see, in short, that when a tax-payer gives his money either to a soldier in exchange for nothing; or to a worker in exchange for something, all the ultimate consequences of the circulation of this money are the same in the two cases; only, in the second case the tax-payer receives something, in the former he receives nothing. The result is—a dead loss to the nation.

The sophism which I am here combating will not stand the test of progression, which is the touchstone of principles. If, when every compensation is made, and all interests satisfied, there is a *national profit* in increasing the army, why not enlist as soldiers the entire male population of the country?

III.—TAXES.

Have you never chanced to hear it said: "There is no better investment than taxes. Only see what a number of families it maintains, and consider how it reacts upon industry: it is an inexhaustible stream, it is life itself."

In order to combat this doctrine, I must refer to my preceding refutation. Political economy knew well enough that its arguments were not so amusing that it could be said of them, *repetitions please*. It has, therefore, turned the proverb to its own use, well convinced that, in its mouth, *repetitions teach*.

The advantages which officials advocate are *those which are seen*. The benefit which accrues to the providers *is still that which is seen*. This blinds all eyes.

But the disadvantages which the tax-payers have to get rid of are *those which are not seen*. And the injury which results from it to the providers is still that *which is not seen*, although this ought to be self-evident.

When an official spends for his own advantage an extra hundred cents, it implies that a tax-payer spends for his profit a hundred cents less. But the expense of the official *is seen*, because the act is performed, while that of the tax-payer *is not seen*, because, alas! he is prevented from performing it.

You compare the nation, perhaps, to a parched tract of land, and the tax to a fertilizing rain. Be it so. But you ought also to ask yourself where are the sources of this rain, and whether it is not the tax itself which draws away the moisture from the ground and dries it up?

Again, you ought to ask yourself whether it is possible that the soil can receive as much of this precious water by rain as it loses by evaporation?

There is one thing very certain, that when James counts a hundred cents for the tax-gatherer, he receives nothing immediately in return. Afterwards, when an official spends three hundred cents and returns them to James, it is for an equal value in corn or labor. The final result is a loss to James of a dollar.

It is very true that often, perhaps very often, the official performs for James an equivalent service. In this case there is no loss on either side; there is merely an exchange. Therefore, my arguments do not at all apply to useful functionaries. All I say is—if you wish to create an office, prove its utility. Show that its value to James, by the services which it performs for him, is equal to what it costs him. But, apart from this intrinsic utility, do not bring forward as an argument the benefit which it confers upon the official, his family, and his providers; do not assert that it encourages labor.

When James gives a hundred cents to a Government officer for a really useful service, it is exactly the same as when he gives a hundred cents to a shoemaker for a pair of shoes.

But when James gives a hundred cents to a

Government officer, and receives nothing for them unless it be annoyances, he might as well give them to a thief. It is nonsense to say that the Government officer will spend these hundred cents to the great profit of *national labor;* the thief would do the same; and so would James, if he had not been stopped on the road by the legal parasite, or by the lawful sponger.

Let us accustom ourselves, then, to avoid judging of things by *what is seen* only, but to judge of them by *that which is not seen.*

Last year I was on the Committee of Finance in the French National Assembly. Every time that one of my colleagues spoke of fixing at a moderate figure the maintenance of the President of the Republic,* that of the ministers, and of the ambassadors, it was answered:—

"For the good of the service, it is necessary to surround certain offices with splendor and dignity, as a means of attracting men of merit to them. A vast number of unfortunate persons apply to the President of the Republic, and it would be placing him in a very painful position to oblige him to be constantly refusing them. A certain style in the ministerial saloons is a part of the machinery of constitutional Governments."

---

* Then Louis Napoleon.

Although such arguments may be despised, they nevertheless deserve a serious examination. They are based upon the public interest, whether rightly estimated or not; and, as far as I am concerned, I have much more respect for them than many of our Catos have, who are actuated by a narrow spirit of parsimony or jealousy.

But what revolts the economical part of my conscience, and makes me blush for the intellectual attainments of my countrymen, is the favorable reception which is almost always accorded to the following proposition: "The luxury of great Government officers encourages the arts, industry, and labor. The head of the State and his ministers cannot give banquets and soirées without causing life to circulate through all the veins of the social body. To reduce their means would starve Parisian industry, and consequently that of the whole nation."

I must beg you, gentlemen, to pay some little regard to arithmetic, at least; and not to say before the National Assembly in France (lest to its shame it should agree with you), that an addition gives a different sum, according to whether it is added up from the bottom to the top, or from the top to the bottom of the column.

For instance, I want to agree with a drainer to make a trench in my field for a hundred sous.

Just as we have concluded our arrangement the tax-gatherer comes, takes my hundred sous, and the national revenue being to this extent augmented, the salary of some great minister is augmented in a like degree. My bargain, however, is at an end, but the minister will have another dish added to his table. Upon what ground will you dare to affirm that this official expense helps the national industry? Do you not see, that in this there is only a reversing of satisfaction and labor? A minister has his table better covered, it is true; but it is just as true that an agriculturist has his field worse drained. A Parisian tavern-keeper has gained a hundred sous, I grant you; but then you must grant me that a drainer has been prevented from gaining five francs. It all comes to this—that the official and the tavern-keeper being satisfied, is *that which is seen;* the field undrained and the drainer deprived of his job, is *that which is not seen.* Dear me! how much trouble there is in proving that two and two make four; and if you succeed in proving it, it is said "the thing is so plain it is quite tiresome," and they keep on legislating in the same old way, as if you had proved nothing at all.

IV.—THEATRES, FINE ARTS.

Ought the State to encourage the arts?

There is certainly much to be said on both sides of this question. It may be said, in favor of the system of voting supplies for this purpose, that the arts enlarge, elevate, and harmonize the soul of a nation; that they divert it from too great an absorption in material occupations; encourage in it a love for the beautiful; and thus act favorably on its manners, customs, morals, and even on its industry. It may be asked, what would become of music in France without her Italian theatre and her Conservatoire; of the dramatic art, without her Théâtre-Français; of painting and sculpture, without our collections, galleries, and museums? It might even be asked whether, without centralization, and consequently the support of the fine arts, that exquisite taste would be developed which is the noble appendage of French labor, and which introduces its productions to the whole world? In the face of such results, would it not be the height of imprudence to renounce this moderate contribution from all her citizens, which, in fact, in the eyes of Europe, demonstrates their superiority and their glory?

To these and many other reasons, whose force I do not dispute, arguments no less forcible may be opposed. It might first of all be said, that there is a question of distributive justice in it. Does the right of the legislator extend to

abridging the wages of the artisan, for the sake
of adding to the profits of the artists? M. Lamartine said, "If you cease to support the theatre,
where will you stop? Will you not necessarily be
led to withdraw your support from your colleges,
your museums, your institutes, and your libraries?"
It might be answered, if you desire to support
everything which is good and useful, where will you
stop? Will you not necessarily be led to make
regular appropriations for agriculture, industry,
commerce, benevolence, education? Then, is it
certain that Government aid favors the progress of
art? This question is far from being settled, and
we see very well that the theatres which prosper
most are those which depend most upon their own
resources. Moreover, if we come to higher considerations, we may observe that wants and desires arise the one from the other, and originate
in regions which are more and more refined in
proportion as the public wealth allows of their
being satisfied; that Government ought not to
take part in this correspondence, because in a certain condition of present fortune it could not by
taxation stimulate the arts of necessity without
checking those of luxury, and thus interrupting
the natural course of civilization. I may observe,
that these artificial transpositions of wants, tastes,
labor, and population, place the people in a pre-

carious and dangerous position, without any solid basis.

These are some of the reasons alleged by the adversaries of State intervention in what concerns the order in which citizens think their wants and desires should be satisfied, and to which, consequently, their activity should be directed. I am, I confess, one of those who think that choice and impulse ought to come from below and not from above, from the citizen and not from the legislator; and the opposite doctrine appears to me to tend to the destruction of liberty and of human dignity.

But, by a deduction as false as it is unjust, do you know what economists are accused of? It is, that when we disapprove of government support, we are supposed to disapprove of the thing itself whose support is discussed; and to be the enemies of every kind of activity, because we desire to see those activities, on the one hand free, and on the other seeking their own reward in themselves. Thus, if we think that the State should not interfere by taxation in religious affairs, we are atheists. If we think the State ought not to interfere by taxation in education, we are hostile to knowledge. If we say that the State ought not by taxation to give a fictitious value to land, or to any particular branch of industry, we are enemies to property and labor. If we think that the State ought not to support artists, we are barbarians, who look upon the arts as useless.

Against such conclusions as these I protest with all my strength. Far from entertaining the absurd idea of doing away with religion, education, property, labor, and the arts, when we say that the State ought to protect the free development of all these kinds of human activity, without helping some of them at the expense of others—we think, on the contrary, that all these living powers of society would develop themselves more harmoniously under the influence of liberty; and that, under such an influence, no one of them would, as is now often the case, be a source of trouble, of abuses, of tyranny, and disorder.

Our adversaries consider that an activity which is neither aided by supplies, nor regulated by government, is an activity destroyed. We think just the contrary. Their faith is in the legislator, not in mankind; ours is in mankind, not in the legislator.

Thus M. Lamartine said: "Upon this principle we must abolish the public exhibitions, which are the honor and the wealth of this country." But I would say to M. Lamartine—According to your way of thinking, not to support is to abolish; because setting out upon the maxim that nothing exists independently of the will of the State, you conclude that nothing lives but what the State causes to live.

To return to the fine arts. There are, I repeat, many strong reasons to be brought, both for and against the system of government assistance. The reader must see that the especial object of this work leads me neither to explain these reasons, nor to decide in their favor, nor against them.

But M. Lamartine has advanced one argument which I cannot pass by in silence, for it is closely connected with this economic study. "The economical question, as regards theatres, is comprised in one word—labor. It matters little what is the nature of this labor; it is as fertile, as productive a labor as any other kind of labor in the nation. The theatres in France, you know, feed and salary no less than 80,000 workmen of different kinds; painters, masons, decorators, costumers, architects, &c., which constitute the very life and movement of several parts of the capital, and on this account they ought to have your sympathies." Your sympathies! say rather your money.

And further on he says: "The pleasures of Paris are the labor and the consumption of the provinces, and the luxuries of the rich are the wages and bread of 200,000 workmen of every description, who live by the manifold industry of the theatres, and who receive from these noble pleasures, which render France illustrious, the sustenance of their lives and the necessaries of their families and children. It is to them that you will give 60,000 francs." (Very well; very well. Great applause.) For my part I am constrained to say, "Very bad! very bad!" confining this opinion, of course, within the bounds of the economical question which we are discussing.

Yes, it is to the workmen of the theatres that a part, at least, of these 60,000 francs will go; a few bribes, perhaps, may be abstracted on the way. Perhaps, if we were to look a little more closely into the matter, we might find that the cake had gone another way, and that those workmen were fortunate who had come in for a few crumbs. But I will allow, for the sake of argument, that the entire sum does go to the painters, decorators, &c.

This is that which is seen. But whence does it come? This is the other side of the question, and quite as important as the former. Where do these 60,000 francs spring from? and where would they go, if a vote of the legislature did not direct them first toward the Treasury and thence toward the theatres? This *is what is not seen.* Certainly, nobody will think of maintaining that the legislative vote has caused this sum to be hatched in a ballot-box; that it is a pure addition made to the national wealth; that but for this miraculous vote these 60,000 francs would have been for ever invisible and impalpable. It must be admitted that all that the majority can do is to decide that they shall be taken from one place to be sent to another; and if they take one direction, it is only because they have been diverted from another.

This being the case, it is clear that the tax-payer, who has contributed one franc, will no longer have this franc at his own disposal. It is clear that he will be deprived of some gratification to the amount of one franc; and that the workman, whoever he may be, who would have received it from him for some service, will be deprived of a benefit to that amount. Let us not, therefore, be led by a childish illusion into believing that the vote of the 60,000 francs may add anything whatever to the well-being of the country, and to national labor. It displaces enjoyments, it transposes wages—that is all.

Will it be said that for one kind of gratification, and one kind of labor, it substitutes more urgent, more moral, more reasonable gratifications and labor? I might dispute this; I might say, by taking 60,000 francs from the tax-payers, you diminish the wages of laborers, drainers, carpenters, blacksmiths, and increase in proportion those of the singers and actors.

There is nothing to prove that this latter class calls for more sympathy than the former. M. Lamartine does not say that it is so. He himself says that the labor of the theatres is *as* fertile, *as* productive as any other (not more so); and this may be doubted; for the best proof that the latter is not so fertile as the former lies in this, that the other is to be called upon to assist it.

But this comparison between the value and the intrinsic merit of different kinds of labor forms no part of my present subject. All I have to do here is to show, that if M. Lamartine and those persons who commend his line of argument have seen on one side the salaries gained by the *providers* of the comedians, they ought on the other to have seen the salaries lost by the *providers* of the tax-payers: for want of this, they have exposed themselves to ridicule by mistaking a *transferment* for a *gain*. If they were true to their doctrine, there would be no limits to their demands for government aid; for that which is true of one franc and of 60,000 is true, under parallel circumstances, of a hundred millions of francs.

When taxes are the subject of discussion, you ought to prove their utility by reasons from the root of the matter, but not by this unlucky assertion—"The public expenses support the working classes." This assertion disguises the important fact, that *public expenses always* supersede *private expenses*, and that therefore we bring a livelihood to one workman instead of another, but add nothing to the share of the working class as a whole. Your arguments are fashionable enough, but they are too absurd to be justified by anything like reason.

V.—PUBLIC WORKS.

Nothing is more natural than that a nation, after having assured itself that an enterprise will benefit the community, should have it executed by means of a general assessment. But I lose patience, I confess, when I hear some one, assuming to occupy a high moral, patriotic, and economic standpoint, assert, "that to authorize the prosecution of public works will be a means of creating opportunity to labor for the workmen."

The State opens a road, builds a palace, straightens a street, cuts a canal, and so gives work to certain workmen—*this is what is seen:* but it deprives certain other workmen of work—and this is what *is not seen*.

The road is begun. A thousand workmen come every morning, leave every evening, and take their wages—this is certain. If the road had not been decreed, if the supplies had not been voted, these good people would have had neither work nor wages there; this also is certain.

But is this all? Does not the operation, as a whole, contain something else? At the moment when the presiding officer announces that the bill authorizing the inception of new public works has become a law, does the money necessary to pay for them descend miraculously on a moonbeam into the national coffers? But in order that the whole scheme may be made complete, must not the State organize the receipts as well as the expenditure? must it not set its tax-gatherers and tax-payers to work, the former to gather and the latter to pay.

Study the question, now, in both its elements. While you state the destination given by the State to the millions voted, do not neglect to state also the destination which the tax-payer would have given, but cannot now give, to the same. Then you will understand that a public enterprise is a coin with two sides. Upon one is engraved a laborer at work, with this device, *that which is seen;* on the other is a laborer out of work, with the device, *that which is not seen.*

The sophism which this work is intended to refute is the more dangerous when applied to public works, inasmuch as it serves to justify the most wanton enterprises and extravagance. When a railway or a bridge are really needed, it is sufficient to demonstrate their necessity to justify an appropriation of the public money for their construction.

But if this immediate necessity cannot be demonstrated, what do the philanthropic patriotic men next say?" "*We must find work for the working men.*"

Public works that under ordinary circumstances would not be thought of are authorized by the public authorities.

The great Napoleon, it is said, thought he was doing a very philanthropic work by causing ditches to be made and then filled up. He said, therefore, "What signifies the result? All we want is to see wealth spread among the laboring classes."

But let us go to the root of the matter. We are deceived by money. To demand the co-operation of all the citizens in a common work, in the form of money, is in reality to demand a co-operation in kind; for every one procures, by his own labor, the sum for which he is taxed. Now, if all the citizens were to be called together, and made to execute, in conjunction, a work useful to all, this would be easily understood; their reward would be found in the results of the work itself.

But after having called them together, if you force them to make roads which no one will pass through, palaces which no one will inhabit, and this under the pretext of finding them work, it would be absurd, and they would have a right to argue, "With this labor we have nothing to do; we prefer working on our own account."

A proceeding which consists in making the citizens co-operate in giving money but not labor does not, in any way, alter the general results. The only thing is, that the loss would react upon all parties. By the former those whom the State employs escape their part of the loss, by adding it to that which their fellow-citizens have already suffered.

There was an article in the Constitution which the Republic of France in 1848 adopted, which read as follows:

"Society favors and encourages the development of labor—by the establishment of public works, by the State, the departments, and the parishes, as a means of employing persons who are in want of work."

As a temporary measure, on any emergency, during a hard winter, this interference with the tax-payers may have its use. It acts in the same way as charity. It adds nothing either to labor or to wages, but it takes labor and wages from ordinary times to give them, at a loss it is true, to times of difficulty.

As a permanent, general, systematic measure, it is nothing else than a ruinous mystification, an impossibility, which shows a little excited labor *which is seen,* and hides a great deal of prevented labor *which is not seen.*

VI.—THE MIDDLE-MEN.

Society is the total of the forced or voluntary services which men perform for each other; that is to say, of *public services* and *private services.*

The former, imposed and regulated by the law, which it is not always easy to change, even when it is desirable, may survive with it their own usefulness, and still preserve the name of *public services,* even when they are no longer services at all, but rather *public annoyances.* The latter belong to the sphere of the will, of individual responsibility. Every one gives and receives what he wishes, and what he can, after he has considered the matter in his own mind. The exchange of private services has always the presumption of real utility, in exact proportion to their comparative value.

This is the reason why the former description of services so often become stationary, while the latter obey the law of progress.

While the exaggerated development of public services, by the waste of strength which it involves, fastens upon society a fatal sycophancy, it is a singular thing that several modern sects, attributing this character to free and private services, are endeavoring to transform professions into functions.

These sects violently oppose what they call intermediates. They would gladly suppress the capitalist, the banker, the speculator, the projector, the merchant and the trader, accusing them of interposing between production and consumption, to extort from both, without giving either anything in return. Or rather, they would transfer to the State the work which they accomplish, for this work cannot be suppressed.

The sophism of the Socialists on this point consists in showing to the public what it pays to the intermediates in exchange for their services, and concealing from the public what it would be necessary to pay to the State for doing the same thing. Here is the usual conflict between what is before our eyes and what is perceptible to the mind only; between *what is seen* and *what is not seen*.

It was at the time of the scarcity in France, in 1847, that the French Socialists attempted and succeeded in popularizing their erroneous theory. They knew very well that the most absurd notions have always a chance with people who are suffering; *malisunda fames*.

Therefore, by the help of the fine words, " trafficking in men by men, speculation on hunger, monopoly," they began to deprecate commerce, and to cast a doubt over its benefits.

"What can be the use," they say, "of leaving to the merchants the care of importing food from the United States and the Crimea? Why do not the State, the departments, and the towns, organize a service for provisions and a magazine for stores? They would sell at a *return price*, and the people, poor things, would be exempted from the tribute which they pay to free, that is, to egotistical, individual, and lawless commerce."

The tribute paid by the people to commerce is *that which is seen*. The tribute which the people would pay to the State, or to its agents, in the Socialist system, is *what is not seen*.

In what does this pretended tribute, which the people pay to commerce, consist? In this: that two men render each other a mutual service, in all freedom, and under the pressure of competition and reduced prices.

When the hungry stomach is at Paris, and grain which can satisfy it is at Chicago, the suffering cannot cease till the grain is brought into contact with the stomach. There are three methods by which this contact may be effected. 1st. The famished men may go themselves and fetch the grain. 2d. They may leave this task to those to whose trade it belongs. 3d. They may club together, and give the office in charge to public functionaries. Which of these three methods possesses the greatest advantages? In every time, in all countries, and the more free, enlightened, and experienced they are, men have *voluntarily* chosen the second. I confess that this is sufficient, in my opinion, to justify this choice. I cannot believe that mankind, as a whole, is deceiving itself upon a point which touches its interest so closely. But let us now consider the subject.

For thirty-six millions of citizens to go and fetch the grain they want from Chicago, is a manifest impossibility. The first method, then, goes for nothing. The consumers cannot act for themselves. They must, of necessity, have recourse to *intermediates*, officials or agents.

But observe, at the same time, that the first of these three methods would be the most natural. In reality, the hungry man has to fetch his grain. It is a task which concerns himself, a service due to himself. If another person, on whatever ground, performs this service for him, takes the task upon himself, this latter has a claim upon him for a compensation. I mean by this to say, that intermediates contain in themselves the principle of remuneration.

However that may be, since we must refer to what the Socialists call a parasite, I would ask, which of the two is the most exacting parasite, the merchant or the official?

Commerce (free of course, otherwise I could not reason upon it), commerce, I say, is led by its own interests to study the seasons, to give daily statements of the state of the crops, to receive information from every part of the globe, to foresee wants, to take precautions beforehand. It has vessels always ready, correspondents everywhere; and it is its immediate interest to buy at the lowest possible price, to economize in all the details of its operations, and to attain the greatest results by the smallest efforts. It is not the French merchants only who are occupied in procuring provisions for France in time of need; and if their interest leads them irresistibly to accomplish their task at the smallest possible cost, the competition which they create amongst each other leads them no less irresistibly to cause the consumers to partake of the profits of those realized savings. The grain arrives: it is to the interest of commerce to sell it as soon as possible, so as to avoid risks, to realize its investments and take advantage of the first opportunity to buy again.

Directed by the comparison of prices, commerce distributes food over the whole surface of the country, beginning always at the highest price, that is, where the demand is the greatest. It is impossible to imagine an organization more completely calculated to meet the interest of those who are in want than the existing organization of commerce, and the beauty of this organization, unperceived as it is by the Socialists, results from the very fact that it is free. It is true, the consumer is obliged to reimburse commerce for the expenses of conveyance, freight, store-rooms, commissions, etc., but can any system be devised in which he who eats grain is not obliged to defray the expenses, whatever they may be, of bringing it within his reach? The remuneration for the service performed has to be paid also; but as regards its amount, this is reduced to the smallest possible sum by competition; and as regards its justice, it would be very strange if the artisans of Paris would not work for the artisans of Marseilles, when the merchants of Marseilles work for the artisans of Paris.

But if, according to the Socialist ideas, the State were to stand in the place of commerce, what would happen? I should like to be informed where the saving would be to the public? Would it be in the price of purchase? Imagine the delegates of 40,000 parishes arriving at Chicago on a given day, and on the day of need: imagine the effect upon prices. Would the saving be in the expenses? Would fewer vessels be required; fewer sailors, fewer teamsters, fewer railways? or would you be exempt from the payment of all these things? Would it be in the profits of the merchants? Would your officials go to Chicago for nothing? Would they travel and work on the principle of fraternity? Must they not live? Must not they be paid for their time? And do you believe that these expenses would not exceed a thousand times the two or three per cent. which the merchant gains, at the rate at which he is ready to treat?

And then consider the difficulty of levying so many taxes, and of dividing so much food. Think of the injustice, of the abuses inseparable from such an enterprise. Think of the responsibility which would weigh upon the Government.

The Socialists, who have invented these follies, and who, in the days of distress, have introduced them into the minds of the masses, take to themselves literally the title of *advanced men;* and it is not without some danger that custom, that tyrant of tongues, authorizes the term, and the sentiment which it involves. *Advanced!* This supposes that these gentlemen can see further than the common people; that their only fault is that they are too much in advance of their age; and if the time is not yet come for suppressing certain parasites on the people, the fault is to be attributed to the public which is in the rear of Socialism.

I say, from my soul and my conscience, the reverse is the truth; and I know not to what barbarous age we should have to go back, if we would find the level of Socialist knowledge on this subject. These modern sectarians incessantly oppose association to actual society. They overlook the fact that society, under a free regulation, is a true association, far superior to any of those which proceed from their fertile imaginations.

Let me illustrate this by an example. Before a man, when he gets up in the morning, can put on a coat, ground must have been enclosed, broken up, drained, tilled, and sown with a particular kind of plant; flocks must have been fed, and have given their wool; this wool must have been spun, woven, dyed, and converted into cloth; this cloth must have been cut, sewed, and made into a garment. And this series of operations implies a number of others; it supposes the employment of instruments for plowing, &c., sheepfolds, sheds, coal, machines, carriages, &c.

If society were not a perfectly real association, a person who wanted a coat would be reduced to the necessity of working in solitude; that is, of performing for himself the innumerable parts of this series, from the first stroke of the pickaxe to the last stitch which concludes the work. But, thanks to the power of association and co-operation, which is the distinguishing characteristic of our race, these operations are distributed amongst a multitude of workers; and they are further subdivided, for the common good, to an extent that, as the consumption becomes more active, one single operation is able to support a new trade.

Then comes the division of the profits, which operates according to the contingent value which each has brought to the entire work. If this is not association, I should like to know what is.

Observe, that as no one of these workers has obtained the smallest particle of matter from nothingness, they are confined to performing for each other mutual services, and to helping each other in a common object, and that all may be considered, with respect to others, *intermediates.* If, for instance, in the course of the operation, the transportation becomes important enough to occupy one person, the spinning another, the weaving another, why should the first be considered a *parasite* more than the other two? The transportation must be made, must it not? Does not he who performs it devote to it his time and trouble? and by so doing does he not spare that of his colleagues? Do these do more or other than this for him? Are they not equally dependent for remuneration, that is, for the division of the produce, upon the law of reduced price? Is it not, in all liberty, for the common good that this separation of work takes place, and that these arrangements are entered into? What do we want with a reformer then, who, under pretense of organizing for us, comes despotically to break up our voluntary arrangements, to check the division of labor, to substitute isolated efforts for combined ones, and to send civilization back? Is association, as I describe it here, in itself less association, because every one enters and leaves it freely, chooses his place in it, judges and bargains for himself on his own responsibility, and brings with him the spring and warrant of personal interest? That it may deserve this name, is it necessary that a pretended reformer should come and impose upon us his plan and his will, and, as it were, to concentrate mankind in himself?

The more we examine these *advanced schools*, the more do we become convinced that there is but one thing at the root of them; ignorance proclaiming itself infallible, and claiming despotism in the name of this infallibility.

VII.—RESTRICTIONS.

Mr. Prohibitionist, who was always talking about the necessity of fostering domestic industry, devoted his time and capital to converting the ore found on his land into iron. As nature had been more lavish towards the Belgians, they furnished the French with iron cheaper than Mr. Prohibitionist; which means, that all the French, or France, could obtain a given quantity of iron with less labor by buying it of the honest Flemings. Therefore, guided by their own interest, they did not fail to do so; and every day there might be seen a multitude of nail-smiths, blacksmiths, cartwrights, machinists, farriers, and laborers, going themselves, or sending intermediates, to supply themselves in Belgium. This displeased Mr. Prohibitionist and his friends exceedingly.

At first, it occurred to him to put an end to this abuse by his own efforts: it was the least he could do, for he was the only sufferer. "I will take my gun," said he; "I will put four pistols into my belt; I will fill my cartridge box; I will gird on my sword, and go thus equipped to the frontier. There, the first blacksmith, nail-smith, farrier, machinist, or locksmith, who presents himself to do his own business and not mine, I will kill, to teach him how to live." At the moment of starting, Mr. Prohibitionist made a few reflections which calmed down his warlike ardor a little. He said to himself, "In the first place, it is not absolutely impossible that the purchasers of iron, my countrymen and enemies, should take the thing ill, and, instead of letting me kill them, should kill me instead; and then, even were I to call out all my servants, we should not be able to defend the passages. In short, this proceeding would cost me very dear, much more so than the result would be worth."

Mr. Prohibitionist was on the point of resigning himself to his sad fate, that of being only as free as the rest of the world, when a ray of light darted across his brain. He recollected that at Paris there is a great manufactory of laws. "What is a law?" said he to himself. "It is a measure to which, when once it is decreed, be it good or bad, everybody is bound to conform. For the execution of the same a public force is organized, and to constitute the said public force, men and money are drawn from the whole nation. If, then, I could only get the great Parisian law-manufactory to pass a little law, 'Belgian *iron is hereafter prohibited*,' I should obtain the following results:—The Government would replace the few valets that I was going to send to the frontier by 20,000 of the sons of those refractory blacksmiths, farriers, artisans, machinists, locksmiths, nail-smiths, and laborers. Then to keep these 20,000 custom-house officers in health and good humor, it would distribute among them 25,000,000 of francs taken from these blacksmiths, nail-smiths, artisans, and laborers. They would guard the frontier much better; would cost me nothing; I should not be exposed to the brutality of the brokers; should sell the iron at my own price, and have the sweet satisfaction, of seeing our great people thoroughly humbugged. Then they should be encouraged to continually style themselves as promoters of domestic industry, and as always and under all circumstances opposed to competition with the pauper labor of other countries. Oh! it would be a capital joke, and deserves to be tried."

So our friend Prohibitionist went to the law manufactory. Another time, perhaps, I shall relate the story of his underhand dealings, but now I shall merely mention his visible proceedings. He brought the following consideration before the minds of the legislating gentlemen—

"Belgian iron is sold in France at ten francs, which obliges me to sell mine at the same price. I should like to sell at fifteen, but cannot do so on account of this Belgian iron, which I wish was at the bottom of the Red Sea. I beg you will make a law that no more Belgian iron shall enter France. Immediately I will raise my price five francs, and these are the consequences:

"For every hundred-weight of iron that I shall deliver to the public, I shall receive fifteen francs instead of ten; I shall grow rich more rapidly, extend my traffic, and employ more workmen. My workmen and I shall spend much more freely, to the great advantage of our tradesmen for miles around. These latter, having more custom, will furnish more employment to trade, and activity on both sides will increase in the country. This additional sum of money which you will drop into my strong-box, will, like a stone thrown into a lake, give birth to an infinite number of concentric circles of wealth and render everybody embraced by them comfortable and happy."

Charmed with his discourse, delighted to learn that it is so easy to promote, by legislating, the prosperity of a people, the law-makers voted the restriction. "Talk of labor and economy," they said, "what is the use of these painful means of increasing the national wealth, when all that is needed for this object is to pass a law imposing a tax?"

And, in fact, the law produced all the consequences announced by Mr. Prohibitionist: but it is also to be noted, that it produced others which he had not foreseen. To do him justice, his reasoning was not false, but only incomplete. In endeavoring to obtain a privilege, he had taken cognizance of the effects *which are seen*, leaving in the background those *which are not seen*. He had pointed out only two personages, whereas there are three concerned in the affair. It is for us to supply this involuntary or premeditated omission.

It is true, the money, thus directed by law into Mr. Prohibitionist's strong-box, is advantageous to him and to those whose labor it would encourage; and if the Act had caused the money to descend from the moon, these good effects would not have been counterbalanced by any corresponding evils. But unfortunately, the mysterious money does not come from the moon, but from the pocket of a blacksmith, or a nail-smith, or a cartwright, or a farrier, or a laborer, or a shipwright; in a word, from James, who gives it now without receiving a grain more of iron than when he was paying ten francs. Thus, we can see at a glance that this very much alters the state of the case; for it is very evident that Mr. Prohibitionist's *profit* is compensated by James's *loss*, and all that Mr. Prohibitionist can do with the money, for the encouragement of national labor, James might have done himself. The stone has only been thrown upon one part of the lake, because the law has prevented it from being thrown upon another.

Therefore, *that which is not seen* is more important than that *which is seen*, and at this point there remains, as the residue of the operation, a piece of injustice, and, sad to say, a piece of injustice perpetrated by the law!

This is not all. I have said that there is always a third person left in the background. I must now bring him forward, that he may reveal to us a *second loss* of five francs. Then we shall have the entire results of the transaction.

Our former friend James is the possessor of fifteen francs, the fruit of his labor. He is now free. What does he do with his fifteen francs? He purchases some article of fashion for ten francs, and with it he pays (or the intermediate pays for him) for the hundred-weight of Belgian iron. After this he has five francs left. He does not throw them into the river, but (and this is *what is not seen*) he gives them to some tradesman in exchange for some enjoyment; to a bookseller, for instance, for "a History."

Thus, as far as national labor is concerned, it is encouraged to the amount of fifteen francs, viz. :— ten francs for the Paris article, five francs to the bookselling trade.

As to James, he obtains for his fifteen francs two gratifications, viz. :—

1st. A hundred-weight of iron.
2d. A book.

The decree is put in force. How does it affect

the condition of James? How does it affect the national labor?

James pays every centime of his five francs to Mr. Prohibitionist, and therefore is deprived of the pleasure of a book, or of some other thing of equal value. He loses five francs. This must be admitted; it cannot fail to be admitted, that when the restriction raises the price of things, the consumer loses the difference.

But, then, it is said, *national labor* is the gainer.

No, it is not the gainer; for since the Act, it is no more encouraged than it was before, to the amount of fifteen francs.

The only thing is that, since the Act, the fifteen francs of James go to the metal trade, while before it was put in force, they were divided between the milliner and the bookseller.

The violence used by Mr. Prohibitionist on the frontier, or that which he causes to be used by the law, may be judged very differently in a moral point of view. Some persons consider that plunder is perfectly justifiable, if only sanctioned by law. But, for myself, I cannot imagine anything more aggravating. However it may be, the economical results are the same in both cases.

Look at the thing as you will; but if you are impartial, you will see that no good can come of legal or illegal plunder. We do not deny that it affords Mr. Prohibitionist, or his trade, or, if you will, national industry, a profit of five francs. But we affirm that it causes two losses, one to James, who pays fifteen francs where he otherwise would have paid ten; the other to national industry, which does not receive the difference. Take your choice of these two losses, and offset it against the profit which we allow in the first instance. The other will prove not the less a *dead loss.* Here then is the moral: To take by violence is not to produce, but to destroy. Truly, if taking by violence was producing, this country of ours would be a little richer than she is.

VIII.—MACHINERY.

"A curse on machines! Every year their increasing powder devotes millions of workmen to pauperism, by depriving them of work, and therefore of wages and bread. A curse on machines!"

This is a cry which in old times was very common; and is not now wholly unknown.

But to curse machines is to curse the spirit of humanity!

It puzzles me to conceive how any man can feel any satisfaction in such a doctrine.

For, if true, what is its inevitable consequence? That there is no activity, prosperity, wealth, or happiness possible for any people, except for those who are stupid and inert, and to whom God has not granted the fatal gift of knowing how to think, to observe, to combine, to invent, and to obtain the greatest results with the smallest means. On the contrary, rags, mean huts, poverty, and inanition, are the inevitable lot of every nation which seeks and finds in iron, fire, wind, electricity, magnetism, the laws of chemistry and mechanics, in a word, in the powers of nature, an assistance to its natural powers. We might as well say with Rousseau— "Every man that thinks is a depraved animal."

This is not all. If this doctrine is true, since all men think and invent, since all, from first to last, and at every moment of their existence, seek the co-operation of the powers of nature, and try to make the most of a little, by reducing either the work of their hands or their expenses, so as to obtain the greatest possible amount of gratification with the smallest possible amount of labor, it must follow, as a matter of course, that the whole of mankind is rushing towards its decline, by the same mental aspiration towards progress which torments each of its members.

Hence, it ought to be made known, by statistics, that the inhabitants of the United States, abandoning that land of machines, seek for work in Turkey, where they are little used; and, by history, that barbarism helps the progress of civilization, and that civilization flourishes in times of ignorance and barbarism.

There is evidently in this mass of contradictions something which revolts us, and which leads us to suspect that the problem contains within it an element of solution which has not been sufficiently disengaged.

Here is the whole mystery: behind *that which is seen* lies something *which is not seen*. I will endeavor to bring it to light. The demonstration I shall give will only be a repetition of the preceding one, for the problems are one and the same.

Men have a natural propensity to make the best bargain they can, when not prevented by an opposing force; that is, they like to obtain as much as they possibly can for their labor, whether the advantage is obtained from a *foreign producer* or a skilful *mechanical producer*.

The theoretical objection which is made to the exercise of this propensity is the same in both instances. In each instance it is claimed that the exercise of this propensity restricts (at least apparently) the opportunities for labor. But the way to make labor active and in demand, is to freely allow every one to obtain as much as possible for the results of their labor; to use such results as they may see fit; to make the best bargains possible; and the most practical way of preventing men from following their natural propensities in these respects, is to invoke the aid of force and enact restrictions.

Thus, the legislator at one time forbids foreign competition, and at another time the legislators or combinations of individuals forbid mechanical competition.* For what other means can exist for arresting a propensity which is natural to all men, but that of depriving them of their liberty?

---

* When machines for the spinning and weaving of cotton were first introduced into England, the inventors were afraid to work them openly, and their lives were threatened. Subsequently, when the value of the inventions became recognized, Parliament, in order to prevent foreign competition, prohibited, under severe penalties for the violation of the law, the export of any textile machinery, and also the emigration of artificers.

As recently as 1830 agricultural laborers banded together in England, systematically destroyed all the machinery of many farms, down even to the common drills. A newspaper report of the day, says :—" The men conducted themselves with civility ; and such was their consideration, that they moved the machines out of the farm-yards to prevent injury arising to the cattle from the nails and splinters that flew about while the machinery was being destroyed. They could not make up their minds as to the propriety of destroying a horse churn, and therefore that machine was passed over."

Again, as recently as 1873, the rules of the associated masons and bricklayers of New York, would not allow work on the construction of buildings to go on, the contractors of

Nowadays the legislator restricts his opposition to only one of these combinations—the foreign. In old times he was more consistent, for he opposed both.

We need not be surprised at this. On a wrong road, inconsistency is inevitable; if it were not so, mankind would be sacrificed. A false principle never has been, and never will be, carried out to the end.

Now for our demonstration, which shall not be a long one.

James had two dollars, which he had gained by two workmen; but it occurs to him that an arrangement of ropes and weights might be made which would diminish the labor by half. Therefore he obtains the same advantage, saves a dollar and discharges a workman.

He discharges a workman: *this is that which is seen.*

And seeing this only, it is said, "See how misery attends civilization; this is the way that liberty is fatal to equality. The human mind has made a conquest, and immediately a workman is cast into the gulf of pauperism. James may possibly employ the two workmen, but then he will

---

which used machinery for elevating bricks and mortar, in place of having the same carried up in hods, on the shoulders of laborers.

give them only half their wages, for they will compete with each other, and offer themselves at the lowest price. Thus the rich are always growing richer, and the poor, poorer. Society wants remodelling." A very fine conclusion, and worthy of the preamble.

Happily, preamble and conclusion are both false, because behind the half of the phenomenon *which is seen* lies the other half, *which is not seen.*

The dollar saved by James is not seen, no more are the necessary effects of this saving.

Since, in consequence of his invention, James spends only one dollar on hand labor in affecting a result which formerly required the expenditure of two dollars, another dollar remains to him.

If, then, there is in the world a workman with unemployed arms, there is also in the world a capitalist with an unemployed dollar. These two elements meet and combine, and it is as clear as daylight that between the supply and demand of labor, and between the supply and demand of wages, the relation is in no way changed.

The invention and the workman paid with the first dollar now perform the work which was formerly accomplished by two workmen. The second workman, paid with the second dollar, realizes a new kind of work.

What is the change, then, which has taken place? An additional national advantage has been gained; in other words, the invention is a gratuitous triumph—a gratuitous profit for mankind.

From the form which I have given to my demonstration, the following inference might be drawn:—"It is the capitalist who reaps all the advantage from machinery. The working class, if it only suffers temporarily, never profits by it, since, by your own showing, it displaces a portion of the national labor, without diminishing it, it is true, but also without increasing it."

I do not pretend, in this slight treatise, to answer every objection; the only end I have in view, is to combat a vulgar, widely spread, and dangerous prejudice. I want to prove that a new machine only causes the discharge of a certain number of hands, when the remuneration which pays them is abstracted by force. These hands and this remuneration would combine to produce what it was impossible to produce before the invention; whence it follows that the final result is *an increase of advantages for equal labor.*

Who is the gainer by these additional advantages?

First, it is true, the capitalist, the inventor; the first who succeeds in using the machine; and this is the reward of his genius and skill. In this case, as we have just seen, he effects a saving of the expense of production, which, in whatever way it may be spent (and it always is spent), employs exactly as many hands as the machine caused to be dismissed.

But soon competition obliges him to lower his prices in proportion to the saving itself; and then it is no longer the inventor who reaps the benefit of the invention—it is the purchaser of what is produced, the consumer, the public, including the workman; in a word, mankind.

And *that which is not seen* is, that the saving thus procured for all consumers creates a fund whence wages may be supplied, and which replaces that which the machine has exhausted.

Thus, to recur to the forementioned example, James obtains a profit by spending two dollars in wages. Thanks to his invention, the hand labor costs him only one dollar. So long as he sells the thing produced at the same price, he employs one workman less in producing this particular thing, and that is *what is seen;* but there is an additional workman employed by the dollar which James has saved. This is *that which is not seen.*

When, by the natural progress of things, James is obliged to lower the price of the thing produced by one dollar, then he no longer realizes a saving; then he has no longer a dollar to dispose of to procure for the national labor a new production. But then another gainer takes his place, and this gainer is mankind. Whoever buys the thing he has produced, pays a dollar less, and necessarily adds this saving to the fund of wages; and this, again, is *what is not seen.*

Another solution, founded upon facts, has been given of this problem of machinery.

It was said, machinery reduces the expense of production and lowers the price of the thing produced. The reduction of the profit causes an increase of consumption, which necessitates an increase of production; and, finally, the introduction of as many workmen, or more, after the invention as were necessary before it. As a proof of this, printing, weaving, etc., are instanced.

This demonstration is not a scientific one. It would lead us to conclude, that if the consumption of the particular production of which we are speaking remains stationary, or nearly so, machinery must injure labor. This is not the case.

Suppose that in a certain country all the people wore hats. If by machinery, the price could be reduced half, it would not *necessarily follow* that the consumption would be doubled.

Would you say that in this case a portion of the national labor had been paralyzed? Yes, according to the vulgar demonstration; but, according to mine, No; for even if not a single hat more should be bought in the country, the entire fund of wages would not be the less secure. That which failed to go to the hat-making trade would be found to have gone to the economy realized by all the consumers, and would thence serve to pay for all the labor which the machine had rendered useless, and to excite a new development of all the trades. And thus it is that things go on. I have known newspapers to cost ten dollars per annum; now we pay five: here is a saving of five dollars to the subscribers. It is not certain, or at least necessary, that the five dollars should take the direction of the journalist trade; but it is certain, and necessary too, that if they do not take this direction they will take another. One makes use of them for buying in more newspapers; another, to get better living; another better clothes; another, better furniture. It is thus that the trades are bound together. They form a vast whole, whose different parts communicate in secret canals: what is saved by one profits all. It is very important for us to understand *that savings never take place at the expense of labor and wages.**

---

* Charles Knight, in one of his economic publications, also discusses this same question, from the special standpoint of the English laborers who in 1830 broke up and destroyed

IX.—CREDIT.

In all times, but more especially of late years, attempts have been made to extend wealth by the extension of credit.

Now a few are always ready to proclaim that

---

agricultural machinery, with the expectation that by so doing they would increase the opportunity and demand for labor.

It can be fully demonstrated, he says, "that if the English laborers had been successful in their career—had broken all the more ingenious implements which have aided in rendering British agriculture the most perfect in the world—they would not have advanced one step in obtaining more employment or being better paid.

"Thus, we will suppose that the farmer has yielded to this violence; that the violence has had the effect which it was meant to have upon him; and that he takes on all the hands which were out of employ to thrash and winnow, to cut chaff, to plant with the hands instead of with a drill, to do all the work in fact by the dearest mode instead of the cheapest. But he employs just as many as are absolutely necessary, and no more, for getting his corn ready for market, and for preparing in a slovenly way for the seed-time. In a month or two the victorious destroyers discover that not a single hand the more of them is really employed. Why not? There are no drainings going forward, the fences and ditches are neglected, the dung heap is not turned over, the marl is not fetched from the pit; in fact all these labors are neglected which belong to a state of agricultural industry which is brought to perfection. *The farmer has no funds to employ in such labors.* He is paying a great deal more than he paid before for the same, or a less amount of work, because his laborers in the extension and increasing credit is to be found the solution for the whole social problem.

The only basis, alas! of this solution is an optical delusion—if, indeed, an optical delusion can be called a basis at all.

The first thing done is to confuse money with

---

choose to do certain labors with rude tools instead of perfect ones.

"We will imagine that this state of things continues till the next spring. All this while the price of grain has been rising; many farmers have ceased to employ capital at all upon their land. The inventions which enabled them to make a living out of their business being destroyed, they have abandoned the business altogether. A day's work will no longer purchase as much bread as before. The horse, it might be found out, was as great an enemy as the drill-plow; for as the horse will do the field-work of six men, there must be six men employed, without doubt, instead of one horse. But how would the fact turn out? If the farmer still went on, in spite of all these losses and crosses, he might employ men in the place of horses, but not a single man more than the number that would work at the price of the keep of one horse. To do the work of each horse turned adrift, he would require six men; but he would only have about a shilling a day to divide between these six—the amount which the horse consumed.

"As the year advanced, and the harvest approached, it would be discovered that not one-tenth of the land was sown; for although the plows were gone, because the horses were turned off, and there was plenty of labor for those who choose to labor for its own sake, or at the price of horse labor, this amazing employment for human hands some-produce, then paper money (promises to pay money) with actual; and from these two confusions it is pretended that a reality can be drawn.

It is absolutely necessary in this question to forget coin, bills, and the other instruments by means of which productions pass from hand to hand. Our business is with the productions themselves, which are the real objects of the loan; for when a farmer borrows twenty dollars to buy a plow, it is not, in reality, the twenty dollars which are lent to him, but the plow; and when a merchant borrows $20,000 to purchase a house, it is not the $20,000 which he owes, but the house.

---

how would not quite answer the purpose. It has been calculated that the power of horses, oxen, etc., employed in husbandry in Great Britain is ten times the amount of human power. If human power insisted upon doing all the work with the worst tools, the certainty is that not even one-tenth of the land could be cultivated. Where then would all this madness end? In the starvation of the laborers themselves. Even if they were allowed to eat up all they had produced by such imperfect means, they would be just in the condition of other barbarous people, that were ignorant of the inventions that constitute the power of civilization. They would eat up the little corn which they raised themselves, and find they had nothing to give in exchange for clothes, and coal, and candles, and soap, and sugar, and tea, and all the many comforts which those who are now the worst off are not wholly deprived of."—*Knowledge is Power.*

Money only appears for the sake of facilitating the arrangements between the parties.

Peter may not be disposed to lend his plow, but James may be willing to lend his money. What does William do in this case? He borrows money of James, and with this money he buys the plow of Peter.

But, in point of fact, no one borrows money for the sake of the money itself; money is only the medium by which to obtain possession of productions. Now, it is impossible in any country to transmit from one person to another more productions than that country contains.

Whatever may be the amount of real money and of paper money, which is in circulation, the whole of the borrowers cannot receive more plows, houses, tools, and supplies of raw material, than the lenders altogether can furnish; for we must take care not to forget that every borrower supposes a lender, and that what is once borrowed implies a loan.

This granted, what advantage is there in institutions of credit? It is that they facilitate, between borrowers and lenders, the means of finding and treating with each other; but it is not in their power to cause an instantaneous increase of the things to be borrowed and lent. And yet they ought to be able to do so, if the aim of the reformers is to be attained, since they aspire to nothing less than to place plows, houses, tools, and provisions in the hands of all those who desire them.

And how do they intend to effect this?

By making the State security for the loan.

Let us try and fathom the subject, for it contains *something which is seen*, and also *something which is not seen*. We must endeavor to look at both.

We will suppose that there is but one plow in the world, and that two farmers apply for it.

Peter is the possessor of the only plow which is to be had in the country; John and James wish to borrow it. John, by his honesty, his property, and good reputation, offers security. He *inspires confidence;* he has *credit*. James inspires little or no confidence. It naturally happens that Peter lends his plow to John.

But now, according to the Socialist plan, the State interferes, and says to Peter: "Lend your plow to James, I will be security for its return, and this security will be better than that of John, for he has no one to be responsible for him but himself; and I, although it is true that I have nothing, dispose of the fortune of the tax-payers, and it is with their money that, in case of need, I shall pay you the principal and interest." Consequently, Peter lends his plow to James: *this is what is seen*.

And the Socialists rub their hands, and say, "See how well our plan has answered. Thanks to the intervention of the State, poor James has a plow. He will no longer be obliged to dig the ground; he is on the road to make a fortune. It is a good thing for him, and an advantage to the nation as a whole."

Indeed, it is no such a thing; it is no advantage to the nation, for there is something behind *which is not seen*.

It is not seen, that the plough is in the hands of James, only because it is not in those of John.

It is not seen, that if James farms instead of digging, John will be reduced to the necessity of digging instead of farming.

That, consequently, what was considered an increase of loan, is nothing but a displacement of loan. Besides, *it is not seen* that this displacement implies two acts of deep injustice.

It is an injustice to John, who after having deserved and obtained *credit* by his honesty and activity, sees himself robbed of it.

It is an injustice to the tax-payers, who are made to pay a debt which is no concern of theirs.

Will any one say, that Government offers the same facilities to John as it does to James? But as there is only one plow to be had, two cannot be lent. The argument always maintains that, thanks to the intervention of the State, more will be borrowed than there are things to be lent; for the plow represents here the bulk of available capitals.

It is true I have reduced the operation to the most simple expression of it; but if you submit the most complicated Government institutions of credit to the same test, you will be convinced that they can have but one result; viz., to displace credit, not to augment it. In one country, and in a given time, there is only a certain amount of capital available, and all are employed. In guaranteeing payment on the part of the borrowers, the State may, indeed, increase the number of borrowers, and thus raise the rate of interest (always to the prejudice of the tax-payer), but it has no power to increase the number of lenders, and the aggregate amount of the loans.

There is one conclusion, however, which I would not for the world be suspected of drawing. I say, that the law ought not to favor, artificially, the power of borrowing, but I do not say that it ought not to artificially interpose obstacles in the way of borrowing. If, in our system of borrowing on mortgages, or in any other way, there be obstacles to the diffusion of the application of credit, let them be got rid of; nothing can be better or more just than this. But this is all which is consistent with liberty, and it is all that any who are worthy of the name of reformers will ask.

X.—ALGERIA.*

Here are four orators disputing for the platform. First, all the four speak at once; then they speak one after the other. What have they said? Some very fine things, certainly, about the power and the grandeur of France; about the necessity of sowing, if we would reap; about the brilliant future of our gigantic colony; about the advantage of diverting to a distance the surplus of our population, &c., &c. Magnificent pieces of eloquence, and always adorned with this conclusion:—" Vote fifty millions, more or less, for making ports and roads in Algeria; for sending emigrants thither; for building houses and breaking up land. By so doing, you will relieve the French workman, encourage African labor, and give a stimulus to the

---

* In this chapter M. Bastiat discusses a form of public expenditure in France growing out of the colonial policy, adopted by that country, which has no exact counterpart in the fiscal disbursements of the United States. The principles involved in the expenditures of France in behalf of her colony in Algeria, are, however, the same which underlie the expenditures in every country for a great variety of what are called *public purposes;* and therefore, although the illustrations may be foreign and local, the argument admits of universal application.

commerce of Marseilles. It would be profitable every way."

Yes, it is all very true, if you take no account of the fifty millions until the moment when the State begins to spend them; if you only see where they go, and not whence they come; if you look only at the good they are to do when they come out of the tax-gatherer's bag, and not at the harm which has been done, and the good which has been prevented, by putting them into it. Yes, at this limited point of view all is profit. The house which is built in Barbary is *that which is seen;* the harbor made in Barbary is *that which is seen;* the work caused in Barbary is *what is seen;* a few less hands in France is *what is seen;* a great stir with goods at Marseilles is still *that which is seen.*

But, besides all this, there is something *which is not seen.* The fifty millions expended by the State cannot be spent, as they otherwise would have been, by the tax-payers. It is necessary to deduct, from all the good attributed to the public expenditure which has been effected, all the harm caused by the prevention of private expense, unless we say that James would have done nothing with the francs that he had gained, and of which the tax had deprived him; an absurd assertion, for if he took the trouble to earn it, it was because he expected the satisfaction of using it. He would have repaired the palings in his garden, which he cannot now do, and this is *that which is not seen.* He would have manured his field, which now he cannot do, and this is *what is not seen.* He would have added another story to his cottage, which he cannot do now, and this is *what is not seen.* He might have increased the number of his tools, which he cannot do now, and this is *what is not seen.* He would have been better fed, better clothed, have given a better education to his children, and increased his daughter's marriage portion; this is *what is not seen.* He would have become a member of the Mutual Assistance Society, but now he cannot; this is *what is not seen.* On one hand, are the enjoyments of which he has been deprived, and the means of action which have been destroyed in his hands; on the other, are the labor of the drainer, the carpenter, the smith, the tailor, the village schoolmaster, which he would have encouraged, and which are now prevented—all this is *what is not seen.*

Much is hoped from the future prosperity of Algeria; be it so. But the drain to which France is being subjected ought not to be kept entirely out of sight. The commerce of Marseilles is pointed out to me; but if this is to be brought about by means of taxation, I shall always show that an equal commerce is destroyed thereby in other parts of the country. It is said, "There is an emigrant transported into Barbary; this is a relief to the population which remains in the country." I answer, "How can that be, if, in transporting this emigrant to Algiers, you also transport two or three times the capital which would have served to maintain him in France?"*

The only object I have in view is to make it evident to the reader, that in every public expense, behind the apparent benefit, there is an evil which it is not so easy to discern. As far as in me lies, I would make him form a habit of seeing both, and taking account of both.

When a public expense is proposed, it ought to be examined in itself, separately from the pretended encouragement of labor which results from it, for this encouragement is a delusion. Whatever is done in this way at the public expense, private expense would have done all the same; therefore, the interest of labor is always out of the question.

It is not the object of this treatise to criticise

---

* The Minister of War has lately asserted that every individual transported to Algeria has cost the State 8,000 francs. Now it is certain that these poor creatures could have lived very well in France on a capital of 4,000 francs. I ask, how the French population is relieved, when it is deprived of a man, and of the means of subsistence of two men?

the intrinsic merit of the public expenditure as applied to Algeria, but I cannot withhold a general observation. It is, that the presumption is always unfavorable to expenditures which are paid by money raised by taxation. Why? For this reason:—First, justice always suffers from it in some degree. Since James had labored to gain his franc, in the hope of receiving a gratification from it, it is to be regretted that the national treasury should interpose, and take from James this gratification, to bestow it upon another. Certainly, it behoves the treasury, or those who regulate it, to give good reasons for this. It has been shown that the State gives a very provoking one, when it says, "With this franc I shall employ workmen;" for James (as soon as he sees it) will be sure to answer, "It is all very fine, but with this franc I might employ them myself."

Apart from this reason, others present themselves without disguise, by which the debate between the treasury and poor James becomes much simplified. If the State says to him, "I take your franc to pay the police officer who saves you the trouble of providing for your own personal safety; for paving the street which you are passing through every day; for paying the magistrate who causes your property and your liberty to be respected; to maintain the soldier who maintains our frontiers,"—James, unless I am much mistaken, will pay for all this without hesitation. But if the State were to say to him, "I take this franc that I may give you a little prize in case you cultivate your field well; or that I may teach your son something that you have no wish that he should learn; or that the Minister may add another to his score of dishes at dinner; I take it to build a cottage in Algeria, in which case I must take another franc every year to keep an emigrant in it, and another hundred to maintain a soldier to guard this emigrant, and another franc to maintain a general to guard this soldier," &c., &c.,—I think I hear poor James exclaim, " This system of law is very much like a system of cheat!" The State foresees the objection, and what does it do? It jumbles all things together, and brings forward just that provoking reason which ought to have nothing whatever to do with the question. It talks of the effect of this expenditure upon labor; it points to the cook and purveyor of the Minister; it shows an emigrant, a soldier, and a general, living upon the franc; it shows, in fact, *what is seen*, and if James has not learned to take into the account *what is not seen*, James will be duped. And this is why I want to do all I can to impress it upon his mind, by repeating it over and over again.

As the public expenditures displace labor with

out increasing it, a second serious presumption presents itself against them. To displace labor is to displace laborers, and to disturb the natural laws which regulate the distribution of the population over the country. If 50,000,000 francs are allowed to remain in the possession of the tax-payers, since the tax-payers are everywhere, they encourage labor in the 40,000 parishes in France. They act like a natural tie, which keeps every one upon his native soil; they distribute themselves amongst all imaginable laborers and trades. If the State, by drawing off these 50,000,000 francs from the citizens, accumulates them, and expends them on some given point, it attracts to this point a proportional quantity of displaced labor, a corresponding number of laborers, belonging to other parts; a fluctuating population, which is out of its place, and possibly dangerous when the fund is exhausted. Now here is the consequence (and this confirms all I have said): this feverish activity is, as it were, forced into a narrow space; it attracts the attention of all; it is *what is seen*. The people applaud; they are astonished at the beauty and facility of the plan, and expect to have it continued and extended. *That which they do not see* is, that an equal quantity of labor, which would probably be more valuable, has been paralyzed over the rest of France.

XI.—FRUGALITY AND LUXURY.

It is not only in the public expenditure that *what is seen* eclipses *what is not seen*. Setting aside what relates to political economy, this phenomenon leads to false reasoning. It causes nations to consider their moral and their material interests as contradictory to each other. What can be more discouraging or more dismal?

For instance, there is not a father of a family who does not think it his duty to teach his children order, system, the habits of carefulness, of economy, and of moderation in spending money.

There is no religion which does not thunder against pomp and luxury. This is as it should be; but, on the other hand, how frequently do we hear the following remarks:—

" To hoard is to drain the veins of the people."

" The luxury of the great is the opportunity of the little."

" Prodigals ruin themselves, but they enrich the State."

" It is the superfluity of the rich which makes bread for the poor."

Here, certainly, is a striking contradiction between the moral and the social idea. How many eminent spirits, after having moralized over these assertions, repose in peace. It is a thing I never could understand, for it seems to me that nothing can be more distressing than to discover two opposite tendencies in mankind. Why, it comes to degradation at each of the extremes: economy brings it to misery; prodigality plunges it into moral degradation. Happily, these vulgar maxims exhibit economy and luxury in a false light, taking account, as they do, of those immediate consequences *which are seen*, and not of the remote ones, *which are not seen*. Let us see if we can rectify this incomplete view of the case.

Joseph Spendall and Jacob Saveall, after receiving their parental inheritance, have each an income of $10,000. Joseph Spendall practices the fashionable philanthropy. He is what is called a squanderer of money. He renews his furniture several times a year; changes his equipages every month. People talk of his ingenious contrivances to bring them sooner to an end: in short, he surpasses the fast personages who figure in the modern novels.

Thus everybody is singing his praises. It is, "Tell us about Joseph Spendall for ever! He is the benefactor of the workman; a blessing to the people. It is true, he revels in dissipation; he splashes the passers-by; his own dignity and that of human nature are lowered a little; but what of that? He does good with his fortune, if not with himself. He causes money to circulate; he always sends the tradespeople away satisfied. Is not money made round that it may roll?"

Jacob has adopted a very different plan of life. If he is not an egotist, he is, at any rate, an *individualist*, for he considers expense, seeks only moderate and reasonable enjoyments, thinks of his children's prospects, and, in fact, he *economizes*.

And what do people say of him? "What is the good of a rich fellow like him? He is an old skinflint."

There is something dignified in the simplicity of his life; and he is humane, too, and benevolent, and generous, but he *calculates*. He does not spend his income; his house is neither brilliant nor bustling. What good does he do to the jeweler, the carriage-makers, the horse-dealers, and confectioners?

These opinions, which are antagonistic to the practice of prudence, frugality, and morality, are founded on what strikes the eye, namely, the influence of the expenditures of the prodigal; while little or no account is taken of that which does not ostentatiously attract attention, namely, the equal or larger expenditure of the economist.

But things have been so admirably arranged by the Divine inventor of social order, that in this, as in everything else, political economy and morality, far from clashing, agree; and the wisdom of Jacob is not only more dignified, but still more *profitable*, than the folly of Joseph. And when I say profitable, I do not mean only profitable to Jacob, or even to society in general, but more profitable to the workmen themselves—to the trade of the time.

To prove it, it is only necessary to turn the mind's eye to those hidden consequences of human actions which the bodily eye does not see.

Yes, the prodigality of Joseph has visible effects in every point of view. Everybody can see his fine house, his elegant carriage, his superb paintings, his fleet yacht, and his costly attire. Every one knows that his horses run upon the turf. The dinners which he gives attract the attention of the crowds on the avenues; and it is said, "That is a generous man; far from saving his income, he is very likely breaking into his capital." That is *what is seen*.

It is not so easy to see, with regard to the interest of workers, what becomes of the income of Saveall. If we were to trace it carefully, however, we should see that the whole of it, down to the last farthing, affords work to the laborers as certainly as the fortune of Spendall. Only there is this difference: the wanton extravagance of Joseph is doomed to be constantly decreasing, and to come to an end without fail; whilst the wise expenditure of Jacob will go on increasing from year to year. And if this is the case, then, most assuredly, the public interest will be in unison with morality.

Joseph spends upon himself and his household $5,000 a year. If that is not sufficient to content him, he does not deserve to be called a wise man. He is touched by the miseries which oppress the poorer classes; he thinks he is bound in conscience to afford them some relief, and therefore he devotes $2,000 to acts of benevolence. Amongst the merchants, the manufacturers, and the agriculturists he has friends who are suffering under temporary difficulties; he makes himself acquainted with their situation, that he may assist them with prudence and efficiency, and to this work he devotes $2,000 more. Then he does not forget that he has daughters to portion, and sons for whose prospects it is his duty to provide, and therefore he considers it a duty to lay by and put out to interest $2,000 every year.

The following is a list of his expenses:—

1st. Personal expenses $5,000
2d. Benevolent objects.......... 2,000
3d. Offices of friendship 2,000
4th. Saving.................... 2,000

Let us examine each of these items, and we shall see that not a single farthing escapes the national labor.

1st. Personal expenses.—These, as far as workpeople and tradesmen are concerned, have precisely the same effect as an equal sum spent by Spendall. This is self-evident, therefore we shall say no more about it.

2d. Benevolent objects.—The $2,000 devoted to this purpose benefit trade in an equal degree; they reach the butcher, the baker, the tailor, and the carpenter. The only thing is, that the bread, the meat, and the clothing are not used by Jacob, but by those whom he has made his substitutes. Now, this simple substitution of one consumer for another in no way affects trade in general. It is all one whether Jacob spends a dollar or desires some unfortunate person to spend it instead.

3d. Offices of friendship.—The friend to whom Saveall lends or gives $2,000 does not receive them to bury them; that would be against the hypothesis. He uses them to pay for goods, or to discharge debts. In the first case, trade is encouraged. Will any one pretend to say that it gains more by Joseph's purchase of a thoroughbred horse for $2,000, than by the purchase of $2,000 worth of stuffs by Jacob or his friend? For if this sum serves to pay a debt, a third person appears, viz., the creditor, who will certainly employ them upon something in his trade, his household, or his farm. He forms another medium between Saveall and the workmen. The names only are changed, the expense remains, and also the encouragement to trade.

4th. Saving.—There remains now the $2,000 saved; and it is here, as regards the encouragement to the arts, to trade, labor, and the workmen, that Spendall appears far superior to Saveall, although, in a moral point of view, Jacob shows himself in some degree superior to Joseph.

I can never look at these apparent contradictions between the great laws of nature without a feeling of physical uneasiness which amounts to suffering. Were mankind reduced to the necessity of choosing between two parties, one of whom injures his interest, and the other his conscience, we should have nothing to hope from the future. Happily this is not the case; and to see Jacob attain a position of economical superiority, as well as one of moral superiority, it is sufficient to fall back upon this consoling maxim, which is none the less true from having a paradoxical appearance, " To save is to spend."

For what is Jacob's object in saving $2,000? Is it to bury them in his garden? No, certainly; he intends to increase his capital and his income;

consequently, this money, instead of being employed upon his own personal gratification, is used for buying land, a house, &c., or it is placed in the hands of a merchant or a banker. Follow the progress of this money in any one of these cases, and you will be convinced that through the medium of vendors or lenders, it is encouraging labor quite as certainly as if Saveall, following the example of Spendall, had exchanged it for furniture, jewels, and horses.

For when Jacob buys lands or bonds for $2,000, he is determined by the consideration that he does not want to spend this money. This is why you complain of him.

But, at the same time, the man who sells the land or the bonds, is determined by the consideration that he does want to spend the $2,000 in some way; so that the money is spent in any case, either by Jacob or by others in his stead.

With respect to the working class, to the encouragement of labor, there is only one difference between the conduct of Jacob and that of Joseph. Joseph spends the money himself, and around him, and therefore the effect *is seen*. Jacob, spending it partly through intermediate parties, and at a distance, the effect is *not seen*. But, in fact, those who know how to attribute effects to their proper causes, will perceive, that *what is not seen* is as certain as *what is seen*. This is proved by the fact, that in both cases the money circulates, and does not lie in the iron chest of the wise man, any more than it does in that of the spendthrift. It is, therefore, not correct to say that economy does actual harm to trade; as described above, it is equally beneficial with luxury.

But how far superior is it, if, instead of confining our thoughts to the present moment, we let them embrace a longer period!

Ten years pass away. What is become of Joseph and his fortune and his great popularity? Joseph is ruined. Instead of spending $10,000 every year in society, he is, perhaps, a burden to it. In any case, he is no longer the delight of shopkeepers; he is no longer the patron of the arts and of trade; he is no longer of any use to the workmen, nor are his successors, whom he has brought to want.

At the end of the same ten years Jacob not only continues to throw his income into circulation, but he adds an increasing sum from year to year to his expenses. He enlarges the national capital, that is, the fund which supplies wages, and as it is upon the extent of this fund that the demand for laborers depends, he assists in progressively increasing the remuneration of the working class; and if he dies, he leaves children whom he has taught to succeed him in this work of progress and civilization.

In a moral point of view, the superiority of frugality over luxury is indisputable. It is consoling to think that it is so in political economy, to every one who, not confining his views to the immediate effects of phenomena, knows how to extend his investigations to their final effects.

XII.—HE WHO HAS A RIGHT TO LABOR HAS A RIGHT TO THE PROFIT OF LABOR.

"Brethren, you must club together to find me work at your own price." This is the right to work; *i.e.*, elementary socialism of the first degree.

"Brethren, you must club together to find me work at my own price." This is the right to profit; *i.e.*, refined socialism, or socialism of the second degree.

Both of these assumptions live upon such of their effects as *are seen*. They will die by means of those effects *which are not seen*.

That *which is seen* is the labor and the profit excited by social combination. *That which is not seen* is the labor and the profit to which this same combination would give rise, if it were left to the tax-payers.

In France, in 1848, the right to labor for a

moment showed two faces. This was sufficient to ruin it in public opinion.

One of these faces was called *national workshops*. The other was a tax known by the name of *forty-five centimes*. Millions of francs went daily from the national treasury to the national workshops. This was the fair side of the medal.

And this is the reverse. If millions are taken out of a cash-box, they must first have been put into it. This is why the organizers of the right to public labor apply to the tax-payers.

Now, the peasants said: "I must pay forty-five centimes; then I must deprive myself of some clothing. I cannot manure my field; I cannot repair my house."

And the country workmen said: " As our townsman deprives himself of some clothing, there will be less work for the tailor; as he does not improve his field, there will be less work for the drainer; as he does not repair his house, there will be less work for the carpenter and mason."

It was then proved that two kinds of meal cannot come out of one sack, and that the work furnished by the Government was done at the expense of labor, paid for by the tax-payer. This was the termination of the right to labor, which showed itself as much a chimera as an injustice. And yet the right to profit, which is only an exaggeration of the right to labor, is still alive and flourishing.

Ought not the protectionist to blush at the part he would make society play?

He says to it: "You must give me work, and, more than that, lucrative work. I have foolishly fixed upon a trade by which I lose ten per cent. If you impose a tax of twenty per cent. upon my countrymen, and give it to me, I shall be a gainer instead of a loser. Now, profit is my right; you owe it me." Now, any society which would listen to this sophist, burden itself with taxes to satisfy him, and not perceive that the loss to which any trade is exposed is no less a loss when others are forced to make up for it,—such a society, I say, would deserve the burden inflicted upon it.

Thus we learn by the numerous subjects which I have treated, that, to be ignorant of political economy is to allow ourselves to be misled by the immediate effect of a phenomenon; to be acquainted with it is to embrace in thought and in forethought the whole compass of effects.

I might subject a host of other questions to the same test; but I shrink from the monotony of a constantly uniform demonstration, and I conclude by applying to political economy what Chateaubriand says of history:—

"There are," he says, "two consequences in history; an immediate one, which is instantly recognized, and one in the distance, which is not at first perceived. These consequences often contradict each other; the former are the results of our own limited wisdom; the latter, those of that wisdom which endures. The providential event appears after the human event. God rises up behind men. Deny, if you will, the supreme counsel; disown its action; dispute about words; designate by the term force of circumstances, or reason, what the vulgar call Providence; but look to the end of an accomplished fact, and you will see that it has always produced the contrary of what was expected from it, if it was not established at first upon morality and justice."— *Chateaubriand's Posthumous Memoirs.*

GOVERNMENT.

I WISH some one would offer a prize for a good, simple, and intelligent definition of the word "Government."

What an immense service it would confer on society!

The Government! what is it? where is it? what does it do? what ought it to do? All we know is, that it is a mysterious personage; and, assuredly, it is the most solicited, the most tormented, the most overwhelmed, the most admired, the most accused, the most invoked, and the most provoked of any personage in the world.

I have not the pleasure of knowing my reader, but I would stake ten to one that for six months he has been making Utopias, and if so, that he is looking to Government for the realization of them.

And should the reader happen to be a lady, I have no doubt that she is sincerely desirous of seeing all the evils of suffering humanity remedied, and that she thinks this might easily be done, if Government would only undertake it.

But, alas! that poor unfortunate personage, like Figaro, knows not to whom to listen, nor where to turn. The hundred thousand mouths of the press and of the platform cry out all at once :—

"Organize labor and workmen.

"Repress insolence and the tyranny of capital.

"Make experiments upon manure and eggs.

"Cover the country with railways.

"Irrigate the plains.

"Plant the hills.

"Make model farms.

"Found social workshops.

"Nurture children.

"Instruct the youth.

"Assist the aged.

"Send the inhabitants of towns into the country.

"Equalize the profits of all trades.

"Lend money without interest to all who wish to borrow.

"Emancipate oppressed people everywhere.

"Rear and perfect the saddle-horse.

"Encourage the arts, and provide us with musicians, painters, and architects.

"Restrict commerce, and at the same time create a merchant navy.

"Discover truth, and put a grain of reason into our heads. The mission of Government is to enlighten to develop, to extend, to fortify, to spiritualize, and to sanctify the soul of the people."

"Do have a little patience, gentlemen," says Government, in a beseeching tone. "I will do what I can to satisfy you, but for this I must have resources. I have been preparing plans for five or six taxes, which are quite new, and not at all oppressive. You will see how willingly people will pay them."

Then comes a great exclamation:—"No! indeed! where is the merit of doing a thing with resources? Why, it does not deserve the name of a Government! So far from loading us with fresh taxes, we would have you withdraw the old ones. You ought to suppress

"The tobacco tax.
"The tax on liquors.
"The tax on letters.
"Custom-house duties.
"Patents."

In the midst of this tumult, and now that the country has again and again changed the administration, for not having satisfied all its demands, I wanted to show that they were contradictory. But what could I have been thinking about?

Could I not keep this unfortunate observation to myself?

I have lost my character forever! I am looked upon as a man without *heart* and without *feeling* —a dry philosopher, an individualist, a plebeian — in a word, an economist of the practical school. But, pardon me, sublime writers, who stop at nothing, not even at contradictions. I am wrong, without a doubt, and I would willingly retract. I should be glad enough, you may be sure, if you had really discovered a beneficent and inexhaustible being, calling itself the Government, which has bread for all mouths, work for all hands, capital for all enterprises, credit for all projects, oil for all wounds, balm for all sufferings, advice for all perplexities, solutions for all doubts, truths for all intellects, diversions for all who want them, milk for infancy, and wine for old age—which can provide for all our wants, satisfy all our curiosity, correct all our errors, repair all our faults, and exempt us henceforth from the necessity for foresight, prudence, judgment, sagacity, experience, order, economy, temperance, and activity.

What reason could I have for not desiring to see such a discovery made? Indeed, the more I reflect upon it, the more do I see that nothing could be more convenient than that we should all of us have within our reach an inexhaustible source of wealth and enlightenment—a universal physician, an unlimited treasure, and an infallible counselor, such as you describe Government to be. Therefore it is that I want to have it pointed out and defined, and that a prize should be offered to the first discoverer of the phœnix. For no one would think of asserting that this precious discovery has yet been made, since up to this time everything presenting itself under the name of the Government has at some time been overturned by the people, precisely because it does not fulfill the rather contradictory conditions of the programme.

I will venture to say that I fear we are, in this respect, the dupes of one of the strangest illusions which have ever taken possession of the human mind.

Man recoils from trouble—from suffering; and yet he is condemned by nature to the suffering of privation, if he does not take the trouble to work. He has to choose, then, between these two evils. What means can he adopt to avoid both? There remains now, and there will remain, only one way, which is, *to enjoy the labor of others.* Such a course of conduct prevents the trouble and the satisfaction from preserving their natural proportion, and causes all the trouble to become the lot of one set of persons, and all the satisfaction that of another. This is the origin of slavery and of plunder, whatever its form may be—whether that of wars, imposition, violence, restrictions, frauds, &c.—monstrous abuses, but consistent with the thought which has given them birth. Oppression should be detested and resisted—it can hardly be called absurd.

Slavery is disappearing, thank heaven! and, on the other hand, our disposition to defend our property prevents direct and open plunder from being easy.

One thing, however, remains—it is the original inclination which exists in all men to divide the lot of life into two parts, throwing the trouble upon others, and keeping the satisfaction for themselves. It remains to be shown under what new form this sad tendency is manifesting itself.

The oppressor no longer acts directly and with his own powers upon his victim. No, our conscience has become too sensitive for that. The tyrant and his victim are still present, but there is an intermediate person between them, which is the Government—that is, the Law itself. What can be better calculated to silence our scruples, and, which is perhaps better appreciated, to overcome all resistance? We all, therefore, put in our claim, under some pretext or other, and apply to Government. We say to it, "I am dissatisfied at the proportion between my labor and my enjoyments. I should like, for the sake of restoring the desired equilibrium, to take a part of the possessions of others. But this would be dangerous. Could not you facilitate the thing for me? Could you not find me a good place? or check the industry of my competitors? or, perhaps, lend me gratuitously some capital, which you may take from its possessor? Could you not bring up my children at the public expense? or grant me some prizes? or secure me a competence when I have attained my fiftieth year? By this means I shall gain my end with an easy conscience, for the law will have acted for me, and I shall have all the advantages of plunder, without its risk or its disgrace!"

As it is certain, on the one hand, that we are all making some similar request to the Government; and as, on the other, it is proved that Government cannot satisfy one party without adding to the labor of the others, until I can obtain another definition of the word Government I feel authorized to give my own. Who knows but it may obtain the prize? Here it is:

Government *is the great fiction through which everybody endeavors to live at the expense of everybody else.*

For now, as formerly, every one is, more or

less, for profiting by the labors of others. No one would dare to profess such a sentiment; he even hides it from himself; and then what is done? A medium is thought of; Government is applied to, and every class in its turn comes to it, and says, " You, who can take justifiably and honestly, take from the public, and we will partake." Alas! Government is only too much disposed to follow this diabolical advice, for it is composed of ministers and officials—of men, in short, who, like all other men, desire in their hearts, and always seize every opportunity with eagerness, to increase their wealth and influence. Government is not slow to perceive the advantages it may derive from the part which is entrusted to it by the public. It is glad to be the judge and the master of the destinies of all; it will take much, for then a large share will remain for itself; it will multiply the number of its agents; it will enlarge the circle of its privileges; it will end by appropriating a ruinous proportion.

But the most remarkable part of it is the astonishing blindnesss of the public through it all. When successful soldiers used to reduce the vanquished to slavery, they were barbarous, but they were not absurd. Their object, like ours, was to live at other people's expense, and they did not fail to do so. What are we to think of a people who never seem to suspect that *reciprocal plunder* is no less plunder because it is reciprocal; that it is no less criminal because it is executed legally and with order; that it adds nothing to the public good; that it diminishes it, just in proportion to the cost of the expensive medium which we call the Government?

And it is this great chimera which the French nation, for example, placed in 1848, for the edification of the people, as a frontispiece to its Constitution. The following is the beginning of the preamble to this Constitution:—

"France has constituted itself a republic for the purpose of raising all the citizens to an ever-increasing degree of morality, enlightment, and well-being."

Thus it is France, or an abstraction, which is to raise the French to morality, well-being, &c. Is it not by yielding to this strange delusion that we are led to expect everything from an energy not our own? Is it not giving out that there is, independently of the French, a virtuous, enlightened, and rich being, who can and will bestow upon them its benefits? Is not this supposing, and certainly very gratuitously, that there are between France and the French—between the simple, abridged, and abstract denomination of all the individualities, and these individualities themselves—relations as of father to son, tutor to his pupil, professor to his scholar? I know it is often said, metaphorically, "the country is a tender mother." But to show the inanity of such a constitutional proposition, it is only needed to show that it may be reversed, not only without inconvenience, but even with advantage. Would it be less exact to say:

"The French have constituted themselves a Republic to raise France to an ever-increasing degree of morality, enlightenment, and well-being."

Now, where is the value of an axiom where the subject and the attribute may change places without inconvenience? Everybody understands what is meant by this: "The mother will feed the child." But it would be ridiculous to say, "The child will feed the mother."

The Americans formed another idea of the relations of the citizens with the Government when they placed these simple words at the head of their Constitution :—

"We, the people of the United States, for the purpose of forming a more perfect union, of establishing justice, of securing interior tranquillity, of providing for our common defense, of increasing the general well-being, and of securing the benefits of liberty to ourselves and to our posterity, decree," &c.

Here there is no chimerical creation, no *ab-*

straction, from which the citizens may demand everything. They expect nothing except from themselves and their own energy.

If I may be permitted to criticise the first words of the French Constitution of 1848, I would remark, that what I complain of is something more than a mere metaphysical subtilty, as might seem at first sight.

I contend that this *personification* of Government has been, in past times, and will be hereafter, a fertile source of calamities and revolutions.

There is the public on one side, Government on the other, considered as two distinct beings; the latter bound to bestow upon the former, and the former having the right to claim from the latter, all imaginable human benefits. What will be the consequence?

In fact, Government is not maimed, and cannot be so. It has two hands—one to receive and the other to give; in other words, it has a rough hand and a smooth one. The activity of the second is necessarily subordinate to the activity of the first. Strictly, Government may take and not restore. This is evident, and may be explained by the porous and absorbing nature of its hands, which always retain a part, and sometimes the whole, of what they touch. But the thing that never was seen, and never will be seen or conceived, is, that

Government can restore more to the public than it has taken from it. It is therefore ridiculous for us to appear before it in the humble attitude of beggars. It is radically impossible for it to confer a particular benefit upon any one of the individualities which constitute the community, without inflicting a greater injury upon the community as a whole.

Our requisitions, therefore, place it in a dilemma.

If it refuses to grant the requests made to it, it is accused of weakness, ill-will, and incapacity. If it endeavors to grant them, it is obliged to load the people with fresh taxes—to do more harm than good, and to bring upon itself from another quarter the general displeasure.

Thus, the public has two hopes, and Government makes two promises—*many benefits and no taxes*. Hopes and promises, which, being contradictory, can never be realized.

Now, is not this the cause of all our revolutions? For, between the Government, which lavishes promises which it is impossible to perform, and the public, which has conceived hopes which can never be realized, two classes of men interpose—the ambitious and the Utopians. It is circumstances which give these their cue. It is enough if these vassals of popularity cry out to the people: "The authorities are deceiving you; if we were in their place, we would load you with benefits and exempt you from taxes."

And the people believe, and the people hope, and the people make a revolution!

No sooner are their friends at the head of affairs, than they are called upon to redeem their pledge. " Give us work, bread, assistance, credit, instruction, more money," say the people; "and withal deliver us, as you promised, from the demands of the tax-gatherers."

The new *Government* is no less embarrassed than the former one, for it soon finds that it is much more easy to promise than to perform. It tries to gain time, for this is necessary for maturing its vast projects. At first, it makes a few timid attempts. On one hand it institutes a little elementary instruction; on the other, it makes a little reduction in some taxes. But the contradiction is forever starting up before it; if it would be philanthropic, it must attend to its exchequer; if it neglects its exchequer, it must abstain from being philanthropic.

These two promises are for ever clashing with each other; it cannot be otherwise. To live upon credit, which is the same as exhausting the future, is certainly a present means of reconciling them: an attempt is made to do a little good now, at the expense of a great deal of harm in future. But such proceedings call forth the spectre of bankruptcy, which puts an end to credit. What is to be done then? Why, then, the new Government takes a bold step; it unites all its forces in order to maintain itself; it smothers opinion, has recourse to arbitrary measures, ridicules its former maxims, declares that it is impossible to conduct the administration except at the risk of being unpopular; in short, it proclaims itself *governmental.* And it is here that other candidates for popularity are waiting for it. They exhibit the same illusion, pass by the same way, obtain the same success, and are soon swallowed up in the same gulf.

We had arrived at this point, in France, in February, 1849.* At this time the illusion which is the subject of this article had made more way than at any former period in the ideas of the French people, in connection with Socialist doctrines. They expected, more firmly than ever, that *Government,* under a republican form, would open in grand style the source of benefits and close that of taxation. "We have often been deceived," said the people; "but we will see to it ourselves this time, and take care not to be deceived again?"

What could the Provisional Government do? Alas! just that which always is done in similar

---

* This was written in 1849

circumstances—make promises, and gain time. It did so, of course; and to give its promises more weight, it announced them publicly thus:—"Increase of prosperity, diminution of labor, assistance, credit, gratuitous instruction, agricultural colonies, cultivation of waste land, and, at the same time, reduction of the tax on salt, liquor, letters, meat; all this shall be granted when the National Assembly meets."

The National Assembly meets, and, as it is impossible to realize two contradictory things, its task, its sad task, is to withdraw, as gently as possible, one after the other, all the decrees of the Provisional Government. However, in order somewhat to mitigate the cruelty of the deception, it is found necessary to negotiate a little. Certain engagements are fulfilled, others are, in a measure, begun, and therefore the new administration is compelled to contrive some new taxes.

Now, I transport myself, in thought, to a period a few months hence, and ask myself, with sorrowful forebodings, what will come to pass when the agents of the new Government go into the country to collect new taxes upon legacies, revenues, and the profits of agricultural traffic? It is to be hoped that my presentiments may not be verified, but I foresee a difficult part for the candidates for popularity to play.

Read the last manifesto of one of the political parties—which they issued on the occasion of the election of the President. It is rather long, but at length it concludes with these words:—"*Government ought to give a great deal to the people, and take little from them.*" It is always the same tactics, or, rather, the same mistake.

"Government is bound to give gratuitous instruction and education to all the citizens."

It is bound to give "A general and appropriate professional education, as much as possible adapted to the wants, the callings, and the capacities of each citizen."

It is bound "To teach every citizen his duty to God, to man, and to himself; to develop his sentiments, his tendencies, and his faculties; to teach him, in short, the scientific part of his labor; to make him understand his own interests, and to give him a knowledge of his rights."

It is bound "To place within the reach of all, literature and the arts, the patrimony of thought, the treasures of the mind, and all those intellectual enjoyments which elevate and strengthen the soul."

It is bound "To give compensation for every accident, from fire, inundation &c., experienced by a citizen." (The *et cætera* means more than it says.)

It is bound " To attend to the relations of capital with labor, and to become the regulator of credit."

It is bound " To afford important encouragement and efficient protection to agriculture."

It is bound " To purchase railroads, canals, and mines; and, doubtless, to transact affairs with that industrial capacity which characterizes it."

It is bound " To encourage useful experiments, to promote and assist them by every means likely to make them successful. As a regulator of credit, it will exercise such extensive influence over industrial and agricultural associations as shall insure them success."

Government is bound to do all this, in addition to the services to which it is already pledged; and further, it is always to maintain a menacing attitude toward foreigners; for, according to those who sign the programme, "Bound together by this holy union, and by the precedents of the French Republic, we carry our wishes and hopes beyond the boundaries which despotism has placed between nations. The rights which we desire for ourselves, we desire for all those who are oppressed by the yoke of tyranny; we desire that our glorious army should still, if necessary, be the army of liberty."

You see that the gentle hand of Government—

that good hand which gives and distributes, will be very busy under the government of the reformers. You think, perhaps, that it will be the same with the rough hand—that hand which dives into our pockets. Do not deceive yourselves. The aspirants after popularity would not know their trade, if they had not the art, when they show the gentle hand, to conceal the rough one. Their reign will assuredly be the jubilee of the tax-payers.

"It is superfluities, not necessaries," they say, "which ought to be taxed."

Truly, it will be a good time when the exchequer, for the sake of loading us with benefits, will content itself with curtailing our superfluities!

This is not all. The reformers intend that "taxation shall lose its oppressive character, and be only an act of fraternity." Good heavens! I know it is the fashion to thrust fraternity in everywhere, but I did not imagine it would ever be put into the hands of the tax-gatherer.

To come to the details:—Those who sign the programme say, "We desire the immediate abolition of those taxes which affect the absolute necessaries of life, as salt, liquors, &c., &c.

"The reform of the tax on landed property, customs, and patents.

"Gratuitous justice—that is, the simplification

of its forms, and reduction of its expenses." (This, no doubt, has reference to stamps.)

Thus, the tax on landed property, customs, patents, stamps, salt, liquors, postage, all are included. These gentlemen have found out the secret of giving an excessive activity to the *gentle hand* of Government, while they entirely paralyze its *rough hand.*

Well, I ask the impartial reader, is it not childishness, and more than that, dangerous childishness? Is it not inevitable that we shall have revolution after revolution, if there is a determination never to stop till this contradiction is realized:—"To give nothing to Government and to receive much from it?"

If the reformers were to come into power, would they not become the victims of the means which they employed to take possession of it?

Citizens! In all times, two political systems have been in existence, and each may be maintained by good reasons. According to one of them, Government ought to do much, but then it ought to take much. According to the other, this twofold activity ought to be little felt. We have to choose between these two systems. But as regards the third system, which partakes of both the others, and which consists in exacting everything from Government, without giving it anything, it is chimerical, absurd, childish, contradictory, and dangerous. Those who parade it, for the sake of the pleasure of accusing all Governments of weakness, and thus exposing them to your attacks, are only flattering and deceiving you, while they are deceiving themselves.

For ourselves, we consider that Government is and ought to be nothing whatever but the united power of the people, organized, not to be an instrument of oppression and mutual plunder among citizens; but, on the the contrary, to secure to every one his own, and to cause justice and security to reign.

WHAT IS MONEY?

"HATEFUL money! hateful money!" cried F——, the economist, despairingly, as he came from the Committee of Finance, where a project of paper money had just been discussed.

"What's the matter?" said I. "What is the meaning of this sudden dislike to the most extolled of all the divinities of this world?"

F. Hateful money! hateful money!

B. You alarm me. I hear peace, liberty, and life cried down, and Brutus went so far even as to say, "Virtue! thou art but a name!" But what can have happened?

F. Hateful money! hateful money!

B. Come, come, exercise a little philosophy. What has happened to you? Has Crœsus been affecting you? Has Jones been playing you false? or has Smith been libeling you in the papers?"

F. I have nothing to do with Crœsus; my character, by its insignificance, is safe from any slanders of Smith; and as to Jones——

B. Ah! now I have it. How could I be so blind? You, too, are the inventor of a social re-organization—of the *F—— system*, in fact. Your society is to be more perfect than that of Sparta, and, therefore, all money is to be rigidly banished from it. And the thing that troubles you is, how to persuade your people to throw away the contents of their purses. What would you have? This is the rock on which all reorganizers split. There is not one but would do wonders, if he could contrive to overcome all resisting influences, and if all mankind would consent to become soft wax in his fingers; but men are resolved not to be soft wax; they listen, applaud, or reject and—go on as before.

F. Thank heaven I am still free from this fashionable mania. Instead of inventing social laws, I am studying those which it has pleased Providence to invent, and I am delighted to find them admirable in their progressive development. This is why I exclaim, "Hateful money! hateful money!"

B. You are a disciple of Proudhon, then? Well, there is a very simple way for you to satisfy yourself. Throw your purse into the river, only reserving a small draft on the Bank of Exchange.

F. If I cry out against money, is it likely I should tolerate its deceitful substitute?

B. Then I have only one more guess to make. You are a new Diogenes, and are going to victimize me with a discourse on the contempt of riches.

F. Heaven preserve me from that! For riches, don't you see, are not a little more or a little less money. They are bread for the hungry, clothes for the naked, fuel to warm you, oil to lengthen the day, a career open to your son, a certain portion for your daughter, a day of rest after fatigue, a cordial for the faint, a little assistance slipped into the hand of a poor man, a shelter from the storm, a diversion for a brain worn by thought, the incomparable pleasure of making those happy who are dear to us. Riches are instruction, independence, dignity, confidence, charity; they are progress and civilization. Riches are the admirable civilizing result of two admirable agents, more civilizing even than riches themselves— labor and exchange.

B. Well! now you seem to be singing the praises of riches, when, a moment ago, you were loading them with imprecations!

F. Why, don't you see that it was only the whim of an economist? I cry out against money, just because everybody confounds it, as you did just now, with riches, and that this confusion is the cause of errors and calamities without number.

I cry out against it because its function in society is not understood, and very difficult to explain. I cry out against it because it jumbles all ideas, causes the means to be taken for the end, the obstacle for the cause, the alpha for the omega; because its presence in the world, though in itself beneficial, has, nevertheless, introduced a fatal notion, a perversion of principles, a contradictory theory, which, in a multitude of forms, has impoverished mankind and deluged the earth with blood. I cry out against it, because I feel that I am incapable of contending against the error to which it has given birth, otherwise than by a long and fastidious dissertation to which no one would listen. Oh! if I could only find a patient and benevolent listener!

B. Well, it shall not be said that for want of a victim you remain in the state of irritation in which you now are. I am listening; speak, lecture, do not restrain yourself in any way.

F. You promise to take an interest?

B. I promise to have patience.

F. That is not much.

B. It is all that I can give. Begin, and explain to me, at first, how a mistake on the subject of money, if mistake there be, is to be found at the root of all economical errors?

F. Well, now, is it possible that you can conscientiously assure me that you have never happened to confound wealth with money?

B. I don't know; but, after all, what would be the consequence of such a confusion?

F. Nothing very important. An error in your brain, which would have no influence over your actions; for you see that, with respect to labor and exchange, although there are as many opinions as there are heads, we all act in the same way.

B. Just as we walk upon the same principle, although we are not agreed upon the theory of equilibrium and gravitation.

F. Precisely. A person who argued himself into the opinion that during the night our heads and feet changed places, might write very fine books upon the subject, but still he would walk about like everybody else.

B. So I think. Nevertheless, he would soon suffer the penalty of being too much of a logician.

F. In the same way, a man would die of hunger, who having decided that money is real wealth, should carry out the idea to the end. That is the reason that this theory is false, for there is no true theory but such as results from facts themselves, as manifested at all times, and in all places.

B. I can understand, that practically, and under the influence of personal interest, the injurious effects of the erroneous action would tend to correct an error. But if that of which you speak has so little influence, why does it disturb you so much?

F. Because, when a man, instead of acting for himself, decides for others, personal interest, that ever watchful and sensible sentinel, is no longer present to cry out, "Stop! the responsibility is misplaced." It is Peter who is deceived, and John suffers; the false system of the legislator necessarily becomes the rule of action of whole populations. And observe the difference. When you have money, and are very hungry, whatever your theory about money may be, what do you do?

B. I go to a baker's and buy some bread.

F. You do not hesitate about using your money?

B. The only use of money is to buy what one wants.

F. And if the baker should happen to be thirsty, what does he do?

B. He goes to the wine merchant's, and buys wine with the money I have given him.

F. What! is he not afraid he shall ruin himself?

B. The real ruin would be to go without eating or drinking.

F. And everybody in the world, if he is free, acts in the same manner?

B. Without a doubt. Would you have them die of hunger for the sake of laying by pence?

F. So far from it, that I consider they act wisely, and I only wish that the theory was nothing but the faithful image of this universal practice. But, suppose now, that you were the legislator, the absolute king of a vast empire, where there were no gold mines.

B. No unpleasant fiction.

F. Suppose, again, that you were perfectly convinced of this,—that wealth consists solely and exclusively of money, to what conclusion would you come?

B. I should conclude that there was no other means for me to enrich my people, or for them to enrich themselves, but to draw away the money from other nations.

F. That is to say, to impoverish them. The first conclusion, then, to which you would arrive would be this,—a nation can only gain when another loses.

B. This axiom has the authority of Bacon and Montaigne.*

---

* *During the sixteenth and seventeenth centuries this theory was almost universally accepted in Europe.*

F. It is not the less sorrowful for that, for it implies—that progress is impossible. Two nations, no more than two men, cannot prosper side by side.

B. It would seem that such is the result of this principle.

F. And as all men are ambitious to enrich themselves, it follows that all are desirous, according to a law of Providence, of ruining their fellow-creatures.

B. This is not Christianity, but it is political economy.

F. Such a doctrine is detestable. But, to continue, I have made you an absolute king. You must not be satisfied with reasoning, you must act. There is no limit to your power. How would you treat this doctrine—wealth is money?

B. It would be my endeavor to increase, incessantly, among my people the quantity of money.

F. But there are no mines in your kingdom. How would you set about it? What would you do?

B. I should do nothing: I should merely forbid, on pain of death, that a single dollar should leave the country.

F. And if your people should happen to be hungry as well as rich?

B. Never mind. In the system we are discussing, to allow them to export dollars, would be to allow them to impoverish themselves.

F. So that, by your own confession, you would force them to act upon a principle equally opposite to that upon which you would yourself act under similar circumstances. Why so?

B. Just because my own hunger touches me, and the hunger of a nation does not touch legislators.

F. Well, I can tell you that your plan would fail, and that no superintendence would be sufficiently vigilant, when the people were hungry, to prevent the dollars from going out and the grain from coming in.

B. If so, this plan, whether erroneous or not, would effect nothing; it would do neither good nor harm, and therefore requires no further consideration.

F. You forget that you are a legislator. A legislator must not be disheartened at trifles, when he is making experiments on others. The first measure not having succeeded, you ought to take some other means of attaining your end.

B. What end?

F. You must have a bad memory. Why, that of increasing, in the midst of your people, the quantity of money, which is presumed to be true wealth.

B. Ah! to be sure; I beg your pardon. But then you see, as they say of music, a little is enough; and this may be said, I think, with still more reason, of political economy. I must consider. But really I don't know how to contrive——

F. Ponder it well. First, I would have you observe that your first plan solved the problem only negatively. To prevent the dollars from going out of the country is the way to prevent the wealth from diminishing, but it is not the way to increase it.

B. Ah! now I am beginning to see . . . the grain which is allowed to come in . . . a bright idea strikes me . . . the contrivance is ingenious, the means infallible; I am coming to it now.

F. Now, I, in turn, must ask you—to what?

B. Why, to a means of increasing the quantity of money.

F. How would you set about it, if you please?

B. Is it not evident that if the heap of money is to be constantly increasing, the first condition is that none must be taken from it?

F. Certainly.

B. And the second, that additions must constantly be made to it?

F. To be sure.

B. Then the problem will be solved, either negatively or positively; if on the one hand I prevent the foreigner from taking from it, and on the other I oblige him to add to it.

F. Better and better.

B. And for this there must be two simple laws made, in which money will not even be mentioned. By the one, my subjects will be forbidden to buy anything abroad; and by the other, they will be required to sell a great deal.

F. A well-advised plan.

B. Is it new? I must take out a patent for the invention.

F. You need do no such thing; you have been forestalled. But you must take care of one thing.

B. What is that?

F. I have made you an absolute king. I understand that you are going to prevent your subjects from buying foreign productions. It will be enough if you prevent them from entering the country. Thirty or forty thousand custom-house officers will do the business.

B. It would be rather expensive. But what does that signify? The money they receive will not go out of the country.

F. True; and in this system it is the grand point. But to insure a sale abroad, how would you proceed?

B. I should encourage it by prizes, obtained by means of some good taxes laid upon my people.

F. In this case, the exporters, constrained by competition among themselves, would lower their prices in proportion, and it would be like making a present to the foreigner of the prizes or of the taxes.

B. Still, the money would not go out of the country.

F. Of course. That is understood. But if your system is beneficial, the governments of other countries will adopt it. They will make similar plans to yours; they will have their custom-house officers, and reject your productions; so that with them, as with you, the heap of money may not be diminished.

B. I shall have an army and force their barriers.

F. They will have an army and force yours.

B. I shall arm vessels, make conquests, acquire colonies, and create consumers for my people, who will be obliged to eat our corn and drink our wine.

F. The other governments will do the same. They will dispute your conquests, your colonies, and your consumers; then on all sides there will be war, and all will be uproar.

B. I shall raise my taxes, and increase my custom-house officers, my army, and my navy.

F. The others will do the same.

B. I shall redouble my exertions.

F. The others will redouble theirs. In the meantime, we have no proof that you would succeed in selling to a great extent.

B. It is but too true. It would be well if the commercial efforts would neutralize each other.

F. And the military efforts also. And, tell me, are not these custom-house officers, soldiers, and vessels, these oppressive taxes, this perpetual struggle towards an impossible result, this permanent state of open or secret war with the whole world, are they not the logical and inevitable consequence of the legislators having adopted an idea, which you admit is acted upon by no man who is his own master, that "wealth is money; and to increase the amount of money is to increase wealth?"

B. I grant it. Either the axiom is true, and then the legislator ought to act as I have described, although universal war should be the consequence; or it is false; and in this case men, in destroying each other, only ruin themselves.

F. And, remember, that before you became a king, this same axiom had led you by a logical process to the following maxims:—That which one gains, another loses. The profit of one is the loss of the other :—which maxims imply an unavoidable antagonism amongst all men.

B. It is only too certain. Whether I am a philosopher or a legislator, whether I reason or act upon the principle that money is wealth, I always arrive at one conclusion, or one result :—universal war. It is well that you pointed out the consequences before beginning a discussion upon it; otherwise, I should never have had the courage to follow you to the end of your economical dissertation, for, to tell you the truth, it is not much to my taste.

F. What do you mean? I was just thinking of it when you heard me grumbling against money! I was lamenting that my countrymen have not the courage to study what it is so important that they should know.

B. And yet the consequences are frightful.

F. The consequences! As yet I have only mentioned one. I might have told you of others still more fatal.

B. You make my hair stand on end! What other evils can have been caused to mankind by this confusion between money and wealth?

F. It would take me a long time to enumerate them. This doctrine is one of a very numerous family. The eldest, whose acquaintance we have just made, is called the *prohibitive system;* the next, the *colonial system;* the third, *hatred of capital;* the last and worst, *paper money.*

B. What! does paper money proceed from the same error?

F. Yes, directly. When legislators, after having ruined men by war and taxes, persevere in their idea, they say to themselves, "If the people suffer, it is because there is not money enough. We must make some." And as it is not easy to multiply the precious metals, especially when the pretended resources of prohibition have been exhausted, they add, "We will make fictitious money, nothing is more easy, and then every citizen will have his pocket-book full of it, and they will all be rich."

B. In fact, this proceeding is more expeditious than the other, and then it does not lead to foreign war.

F. No, but it leads to civil disaster.

B. You are a grumbler. Make haste and dive to the bottom of the question. I am quite impatient, for the first time, to know if money (or its sign) is wealth.

F. You will grant that men do not satisfy any of their wants immediately with coined dollars, or dollar bills. If they are hungry, they want bread; if naked, clothing; if they are ill, they must have remedies; if they are cold, they want shelter and fuel; if they would learn, they must have books; if they would travel, they must have conveyances—and so on. The riches of a country consist in the abundance and proper distribution of all these things. Hence you may perceive and rejoice at the falseness of this gloomy maxim of Bacon's, "*What one people gains, another necessarily loses:*" a maxim expressed in a still more discouraging manner by Montaigne, in these words: "*The profit of one is the loss of another.*" When Shem, Ham, and Japhet divided amongst themselves the vast solitudes of this earth, they surely might each of them build, drain, sow, reap, and obtain improved lodging, food and clothing, and better instruction, perfect and enrich themselves—in short, increase their enjoyments, without causing a necessary diminution in the corresponding enjoyments of their brothers. It is the same with two nations.

B. There is no doubt that two nations, the same as two men, unconnected with each other, may, by working more, and working better, prosper at the same time, without injuring each other. It is not this which is denied by the axioms of Montaigne and Bacon. They only mean to say, that in the transactions which take place between two nations or two men, if one gains, the other must lose. And this is self-evident, as exchange adds nothing by itself to the mass of those useful things of which you were speaking; for if, after the exchange, one of the parties is found to have gained something, the other will, of course, be found to have lost something.

F. You have formed a very incomplete, nay, a false idea of exchange. If Shem is located upon a plain which is fertile in corn, Japhet upon a slope adapted for growing the vine, Ham upon a rich pasturage—the distinction of their occupations, far from hurting any of them, might cause all three to prosper more. It must be so, in fact, for the distribution of labor, introduced by exchange, will have the effect of increasing the mass of corn, wine, and meat which is produced, and which is to be shared. How can it be otherwise, if you allow liberty in these transactions? From the moment that any one of the brothers should perceive that labor in company, as it were, was a permanent loss, compared to solitary labor, he would cease to exchange. Exchange brings with it its claim to our gratitude. The fact of its being accomplished proves that it is a good thing.

B. But Bacon's axiom is true in the case of gold and silver. If we admit that at a certain moment there exists in the world a given quantity, it is perfectly clear that one purse cannot be filled without another being emptied.

F. And if gold is considered to be riches, the

natural conclusion is, that displacements of fortune take place among men, but no general progress. It is just what I said when I began. If, on the contrary, you look upon an abundance of useful things, fit for satisfying our wants and our tastes, as true riches, you will see that simultaneous prosperity is possible. Money serves only to facilitate the transmission of these useful things from one to another, which may be done equally well with an ounce of rare metal like gold, with a pound of more abundant material as silver, or with a hundredweight of still more abundant metal, as copper. According to that, if a country like the United States had at its disposal as much again of all these useful things, its people would be twice as rich, although the quantity of money remained the same; but it would not be the same if there were double the money, for in that case the amount of useful things would not increase.

B. The question to be decided is, whether the presence of a greater number of dollars has not the effect, precisely, of augmenting the sum of useful things?

F. What connection can there be between these two terms? Food, clothing, houses, fuel, all come from nature and from labor, from more or less skillful labor exerted upon a more or less liberal nature.

B. You are forgetting one great force, which is—exchange. If you acknowledge that this is a force, as you have admitted that dollars facilitate it, you must also allow that they have an indirect power of production.

F. But I have added, that a small quantity of rare metal facilitates transactions as much as a large quantity of abundant metal; whence it follows, that a people is not enriched by being *forced* to give up useful things for the sake of having more money.

B. Thus, it is your opinion that the treasures discovered in California will not increase the wealth of the world?

F. I do not believe that, on the whole, they will add much to the enjoyments, to the real satisfactions of mankind. If the Californian gold merely replaces in the world that which has been lost and destroyed, it may have its use. If it increases the amount of money, it will depreciate it. The gold diggers will be richer than they would have been without it. But those in whose possession the gold is at the moment of its depreciation, will obtain a smaller gratification for the same amount. I cannot look upon this as an increase, but as a displacement of true riches, as I have defined them.

B. All that is very plausible. But you will not easily convince me that I am not richer (all other things being equal) if I have two dollars, than if I had only one.

F. I do not deny it.

B. And what is true of me is true of my neighbor, and of the neighbor of my neighbor, and so on, from one to another, all over the country. Therefore, if every citizen of the United States has more dollars, the United States must be more rich.

F. And here you fall into the common mistake of concluding that what affects one affects all, and thus confusing the individual with the general interest.

B. Why, what can be more conclusive? What is true of one, must be so of all. What are all, but a collection of individuals? You might as well tell me that every American could suddenly grow an inch taller, without the average height of all the Americans being increased.

F. Your reasoning is apparently sound, I grant you, and that is why the allusion it conceals is so common. However, let us examine it a little. Ten persons were at play. For greater ease, they had adopted the plan of each taking ten counters, and against these they each placed a hundred dollars under a candlestick, so that each counter corresponded to ten dollars. After the game the winnings were adjusted, and the players drew from the candlestick as many ten dollars as would represent the number of counters. Seeing this, one of them, a great arithmetician perhaps, but an indifferent reasoner, said: "Gentlemen, experience invariably teaches me that, at the end of the game, I find myself a gainer in proportion to the number of my counters. Have you not observed the same with regard to yourselves? Thus, what is true of me must be true of each of you, and *what is true of each must be true of all*. We should, therefore, all of us gain more, at the end of the game, if we all had more counters. Now, nothing can be easier; we have only to distribute twice the number of counters." This was done; but when the game was finished, and they came to adjust the winnings, it was found that the one ~~thousand~~ under the candlestick had not been miraculously multiplied, according to the general expectation. They had to be divided accordingly, and the only result obtained (chimerical enough) was this;—every one had, it is true, his double number of counters, but every counter, instead of corresponding to *ten* dollars, only represented *five*. Thus it was clearly shown that what is true of each is not always true of all.

B. I see; you are supposing a general increase of counters, without a corresponding increase of the sum placed under the candlestick.

F. And you are supposing a general increase of dollars, without a corresponding increase of things, the exchange of which is facilitated by these dollars.

B. Do you compare the dollars to counters?

F. In any other point of view, certainly not; but in the case you place before me, and which I have to argue against, I do. Remark one thing. In order that there be a general increase of dollars in a country, this country must have mines, or its commerce must be such as to give useful things in exchange for money. Apart from these two circumstances, a universal increase is impossible, the dollars only changing hands; and in this case, although it may be very true that each one, taken individually, is richer in proportion to the number of dollars that he has, we cannot draw the inference which you drew just now, because a dollar more in one purse implies necessarily a dollar less in some other. It is the same as with your comparison of the middle height. If each of us grew only at the expense of others, it would be very true of each, taken individually, that he would be a taller man if he had the chance, but this would never be true of the whole taken collectively.

B. Be it so: but, in the two suppositions that you have made, the increase is real, and you must allow that I am right.

F. To a certain point, gold and silver have a value. To obtain this value, men consent to give other useful things which have a value also. When, therefore, there are mines in a country, if that country obtains from them sufficient gold to purchase a useful thing from abroad—a locomotive, for instance—it enriches itself with all the enjoyments which a locomotive can procure, exactly as if the machine had been made at home. The question is, whether it spends more efforts in the former proceeding than in the latter? For if it did not export this gold, it would depreciate, and something worse would happen than what did sometimes happen in California and in Australia, for there, at least, the precious metals are used to buy useful things made elsewhere. Nevertheless, there is still a danger that they may starve on heaps of gold; as it would be if the law prohibited the exportation of gold. As to the second supposition—that of the gold which we obtain by trade: it is an advantage, or the reverse, according as the country stands more or less in need of it, compared to its wants of the useful things which must be given up in order to obtain it. It is not for the law to judge of this, but for those who are concerned in it; for if the law should start upon this principle, that gold is preferable to useful things, whatever may be their value, and if it should act effectually in this sense, it would tend to put every country adopting the law in the curious position of having a great deal of cash to spend, and nothing to buy. It is the very same system which is represented by Midas, who turned everything he touched into gold, and was in consequence in danger of dying of starvation.

B. The gold which is *im*ported implies that a *useful thing* is *ex*ported, and in this respect there is a satisfaction withdrawn from the country. But is there not a corresponding benefit? And will not this gold be the source of a number of new satisfactions, by circulating from hand to hand, and inciting to labor and industry, until at length it leaves the country in its turn, and causes the importation of some useful thing?

F. Now you have come to the heart of the question. Is it true that a dollar is the principle which causes the production of all the objects whose exchange it facilitates? It is very clear that a piece of coined gold or silver stamped as a dollar is only worth a dollar; but we are led to believe that this value has a particular character: that it is not consumed like other things, or that it is exhausted very gradually; that it renews itself, as it were, in each transaction; and that, finally this particular dollar has been worth a dollar, as many times as it has accomplished transactions—that it is of itself worth all the things for which it has been successively exchanged; and this is believed, because it is supposed that without this dollar these things would never have been produced. It is said the shoemaker would have sold fewer shoes, consequently he would have bought less of the butcher; the butcher would not have gone so often to the grocer, the grocer to the doctor, the doctor to the lawyer, and so on.

B. No one can dispute that.

F. This is the time, then, to analyze the true function of money, independently of mines and importations. You have a dollar. What does it imply in your hands? It is, as it were, the witness and proof that you have, at some time or other, performed some labor, which, instead of turning to your advantage, you have bestowed upon society as represented by the person of your client (employer or debtor). This coin testifies that you have performed a *service* for society, and, moreover, it shows the value of it. It bears witness, besides, that you have not yet obtained from society a *real* equivalent service, to which you have a right. To place you in a condition to exercise this right, at the time and in the manner you please, society, as represented by your client, has given you an acknowledgment, a title, a privilege from the republic, a counter, a title to a dollar's worth of property in fact, which only differs from executive titles by bearing its value in itself; and if you are able to read with your mind's eye the inscriptions stamped upon it you will distinctly decipher these words: —*"Pay the bearer a service equivalent to what he has rendered to society, the value received being shown, proved, and measured by that which is represented by me."* Now, you give up your dollar to me. Either my title to it is gratuitous, or it is a claim. If you give it me as payment for a service, the following is the result:—your account with society for real satisfactions is regulated, balanced, and closed. You had rendered it a service for a dollar, you now restore the dollar for a service; as far as you are concerned you are clear. As for me, I am just in the position in which you were just now. It is I who am now in advance to society for the service which I have just rendered it in your person. I am become its creditor for the value of the labor which I have performed for you, and which I might devote to myself. It is into my hands, then, that the title of this credit—the proof of this social debt—ought to pass. You cannot say that I am any richer; if I am entitled to receive, it is because

I have given. Still less can you say that society is a dollar richer, because one of its members has a dollar more, and another has one less. For if you let me have this dollar gratis, it is certain that I shall be so much the richer, but you will be so much the poorer for it; and the social fortune, taken in a mass, will have undergone no change, because as I have already said, this fortune consists in real services, in effective satisfactions, in useful things. You were a creditor to society; you made me a substitute to your rights, and it signifies little to society, which owes a service, whether it pays the debt to you or to me. This is discharged as soon as the bearer of the claim is paid.

B. But if we all had a great number of dollars we should obtain from society many services. Would not that be very desirable?

F. You forget that in the process which I have described, and which is a picture of the reality, we only obtain services from society because we have bestowed some upon it. Whoever speaks of a *service*, speaks, at the same time of a service *received* and *returned,* for these two terms imply each other, so that the one must always be balanced by the other. It is impossible for society to render more services than it receives, and yet a belief to the contrary is the chimera which is being pursued by means of the multiplication of coins, of paper money, etc.

B. All that appears very reasonable in theory, but in practice I cannot help thinking, when I see how things go, that if, by some fortunate circumstance, the number of dollars could be multiplied in such a way that each of us could see his little property doubled, we should all be more at our ease; we should all make more purchases, and trade would receive a powerful stimulus.

F. More purchases! and what should we buy? Doubtless, useful articles—things likely to procure for us substantial gratification—such as provisions, stuffs, houses, books, pictures. You should begin, then, by proving that all these things create themselves; you must suppose the Mint melting ingots of gold which have fallen from the moon; or that the printing presses be put in action at the Treasury Department; for you cannot reasonably think that if the quantity of corn, cloth, ships, hats, and shoes remains the same, the share of each of us can be greater, because we each go to market with a greater amount of real or fictitious money. Remember the players. In the social order the useful things are what the workers place under the candlestick, and the dollars which circulate from hand to hand are the counters. If you multiply the dollars without multiplying the useful things, the only result will be that more dollars will be required for each exchange, just as the players required more counters for each deposit. You have the proof of this in what passes for gold, silver, and copper. Why does the same exchange require more copper than silver, more silver than gold? Is it not because these metals are distributed in the world in different proportions? What reason have you to suppose that if gold were suddenly to become as abundant as silver, it would not require as much of one as of the other to buy a house?

B. You may be right, but I should prefer your being wrong. In the midst of the sufferings which surround us, so distressing in themselves, and so dangerous in their consequences, I have found some consolation in thinking that there was an easy method of making all the members of the community happy.

F. Even if gold and silver were true riches, it would be no easy matter to increase the amount of them in a country where there are no mines.

B. No, but it is easy to substitute something else. I agree with you that gold and silver can do but little service, except as a mere means of exchange. It is the same with paper money, bank-notes, etc. Then, if we had all of us plenty of the latter, which it is so easy to create, we might all buy a great deal, and should want for nothing.* Your cruel theory dissipates hopes, illusions, if you will, whose principle is assuredly very philanthropic.

F. Yes, like all other barren dreams formed to promote universal felicity. The extreme facility

---

* Stated in the abstract, these views, which M. Bastiat causes his imaginary advocate of the issue and use of irredeemable paper money to express, seem so absurd, that one reading involuntarily asks himself: "Do people in actual life, holding important positions of trust and influence really ever thus talk and believe?" To this the answer, unfortunately, must be in the affirmative. The legislative history of all countries is full of examples of such utterances; and that of the United States, especially, abounds with them, Pelatiah Webster, in his history of "Continental Money," tells us that when the subject of increased taxation for the support of the war was under consideration by the Continental Congress, a member arose and indignantly asked, "if he was expected to help tax people, when they could go to the printing-office and get money by the cart load."

During the debates in the Senate of the United States in 1875, the Hon. O. P. Morton, a senator from Indiana, a man whom no small number of people have thought worthy of being called to the Executive chair of the nation, authoritatively laid down this proposition: "*That an abundance of money*" (meaning irredeemable paper money) "*does produce enterprise, prosperity, and progress; that when money was plentiful interest would be lower,*" *just as when horses and hogs are abundant, horses and hogs are cheap.* The trouble of the means which you recommend is quite sufficient to expose its hollowness. Do you believe that if it were merely needful to print bank-notes in order to satisfy all our wants, our tastes, and desires, that mankind would have been contented to go on till now without having recourse to this plan? I agree with you that the discovery is tempting. It would immediately banish from the world, not only plunder, in its diversified and deplorable forms, but even labor itself, except in the National Printing Bureau. But we have yet to learn how greenbacks are to purchase houses, which no one would have built; corn, which no one would have raised; stuffs, which no one would have taken the trouble to weave.

B. One thing strikes me in your argument. You say yourself that if there is no gain, at any rate there is no loss in multiplying the instrument of exchange, as is seen by the instance of the players, who were quits by a very mild deception. Why, then, refuse the philosopher's stone, which

---

here was that this senator had not sufficiently comprehended the a, b, c's of finance, to appreciate the difference between capital and currency; and in the simplicity of his heart imagined that it was all the same whether we had pictures of horses, hogs, and money, or real horses, hogs, and money, which represent, and are only produced by labor.—*Robinson Crusoe's Money*, p. 110.

would teach us the secret of changing base material into gold, or what is the same thing, converting paper into money ? Are you so blindly wedded to your logic, that you would refuse to try an experiment where there can be no risk ? If you are mistaken, you are depriving the nation, as your numerous adversaries believe, of an immense advantage. If the error is on their side, no harm can result, as you yourself say, beyond the failure of a hope. The measure, excellent in their opinion, in yours is merely negative. Let it be tried, then, since the worst which can happen is not the realization of an evil, but the non-realization of a benefit.

F. In the first place, the failure of a hope is a very great misfortune to any people. It is also very undesirable that the government should announce the abolition of several taxes on the faith of a resource which must infallibly fail. Nevertheless, your remark would deserve some consideration, if, after the issue of paper money and its depreciation, the equilibrium of values should instantly and simultaneously take place in all things and in every part of the country. The measure would tend, as in my example of the players, to a universal mystification, in respect to which the best thing we could do would be to look at one another and laugh. But this is not in the course of events. The experiment has been made, and every time a government—be it King or Congress—has altered the money . . .

B. Who says anything about altering the money?

F. Why, to force people to take in payment scraps of paper which have been officially baptized *dollars*, or to force them to receive, as weighing an ounce, a piece of silver which weighs only half an ounce, but which has been officially named a *dollar*, is the same thing, if not worse; and all the reasoning which can be made in favor of paper money has been made in favor of legal false-coined money. Certainly, looking at it, as you did just now, and as you appear to be doing still, if it is believed that to multiply the instruments of exchange is to multiply the exchanges themselves as well as the things exchanged, it might very reasonably be thought that the most simple means was to mechanically divide the coined dollar, and to cause the law to give to the half the name and value of the whole. Well, in both cases, depreciation is inevitable. I think I have told you the cause. I must also inform you, that this depreciation, which, with paper, might go on till it came to nothing, is effected by continually making dupes; and of these, poor people, simple persons, workmen and countrymen are the chief.

B. I see; but stop a little. This dose of Economy is rather too strong for once.

F. Be it so. We are agreed, then, upon this point—that wealth is the mass of useful things which we produce by labor; or, still better, the result of all the efforts which we make for the satisfaction of our wants and tastes. These useful things are exchanged for each other, according to the convenience of those to whom they belong. There are two forms in these transactions; one is called barter: in this case a service is rendered for the sake of receiving an equivalent service immediately. In this form transactions would be exceedingly limited. In order that they may be multiplied, and accomplished independently of time and space amongst persons unknown to each other, and by infinite fractions, an intermediate agent has been necessary—this is money. It gives occasion for exchange, which is nothing else but a complicated bargain. This is what has to be remarked and understood. Exchange decomposes itself into two bargains, into two departments, sale and purchase—the reunion of which is needed to complete it. You *sell* a service, and receive a dollar—then, with this dollar you *buy* a service. Then only is the bargain complete; it is not till then that your effort has been followed by a real satisfaction. Evidently you only work to satisfy the wants of others, that others may work to satisfy yours. So long as you have only the dollar which has been given you for your work, you are only entitled to claim the work of another person. When you have done so, the economical evolution will be accomplished as far as you are concerned, since you will then only have obtained, by a real satisfaction, the true reward for your trouble. The idea of a bargain implies a service rendered, and a service received. Why should it not be the same with exchange, which is merely a bargain in two parts? And here there are two observations to be made. First—It is a very unimportant circumstance whether there be much or little money in the world. If there is much, much is required; if there is little, little is wanted, for each transaction: that is all. The second observation is this:—Because it is seen that money always reappears in every exchange, it has come to be regarded as the *sign* and the *measure* of the things exchanged.

B. Will you still deny that money is the *sign* of the useful things of which you speak?

F. A half-eagle is no more the sign of a barrel of flour, than a barrel of flour is the sign of a half-eagle.

B. What harm is there in looking at money as the sign of wealth?

F. The inconvenience is this—it leads to the

idea that we have only to increase the sign, in order to increase the things signified; and we are in danger of adopting all the false measures which you took when I made you an absolute king. We should go still further. Just as in money we see the sign of wealth, we see also in paper money the sign of money; and thence conclude that there is a very easy and simple method of procuring for everybody the pleasures of fortune.

B. But you will not go so far as to dispute that money is the *measure* of values?

F. Yes, certainly, I do go as far as that, for that is precisely where the illusion lies. It has become customary to refer the value of everything to that of money. It is said, this is *worth* five, ten, or twenty dollars, as we say this *weighs* five, ten, or twenty grains; this *measures* five, ten, or twenty yards; this ground *contains* five, ten, or twenty acres; and hence it has been concluded that money is the *measure* of *values*.

B. Well, it appears as if it was so.

F. Yes, it appears so, and it is this appearance I complain of, and not of the reality. A measure of length, size, surface, is a quantity agreed upon, and unchangeable. It is not so with the value of gold and silver. This varies as much as that of corn, wine, cloth, or labor, and from the same causes, for it has the same source and obeys the same laws. Gold is brought within our reach, just like iron, by the labor of miners, the advances of capitalists, and the combination of merchants and seamen. It costs more or less, according to the expense of its production, according to whether there is much or little in the market, and whether it is much or little in request; in a word, it undergoes the fluctuations of all other human productions. But one circumstance is singular, and gives rise to many mistakes. When the value of money varies, the variation is attributed by language to the other productions for which it is exchanged. Thus, let us suppose that all the circumstances relative to gold remain the same, and that the corn harvest has failed. The price of corn will rise. It will be said, "The barrel of flour, which was worth five dollars, is now worth eight;" and this will be correct, for it is the value of the flour which has varied, and language agrees with the fact. But let us reverse the supposition: let us suppose that all the circumstances relative to flour remain the same, and that half of all the gold in existence is swallowed up; this time it is the price of gold which will rise. It would seem that we ought to say, "This half-eagle, which *was worth* ten dollars, *is now worth* twenty." Now, do you know how this is expressed? Just as if it was the other objects of comparison which had fallen in price, it is said—" Flour, which *was worth* ten dollars, *is now only worth* five."

B. It all comes to the same thing in the end.

F. No doubt; but only think what disturbances, what cheatings are produced in exchanges, when the value of the medium varies, without our becoming aware of it by a change in the name. Old pieces are issued, or notes bearing the name of five dollars, and which will bear that name through every subsequent depreciation. The value will be reduced a quarter, a half, but they will still be called *pieces* or *notes of five dollars.* Clever persons will take care not to part with their goods unless for a larger number of notes—in other words, they will ask ten dollars for what they would formerly have sold for five; but simple persons will be taken in. Many years must pass before all the values will find their proper level. Under the influence of ignorance and *custom*, the day's pay of a country laborer will remain for a long time at a dollar while the salable price of all the articles of consumption around him will be rising. He will sink into destitution without being able to discover the cause. In short, since you wish me to finish, I must beg you, before we separate, to fix your whole attention upon this essential point:—When once false money (under whatever form it may take) is put into circulation, depreciation will ensue, and manifest itself by the universal rise of every thing which is capable of being sold. But this rise in prices is not instantaneous and equal for all things. Sharp men, brokers, and men of business, will not suffer by it; for it is their trade to watch the fluctuations of prices, to observe the cause, and even to speculate upon it. But little tradesmen, countrymen, and workmen will bear the whole weight of it. The rich man is not any the richer for it, but the poor man becomes poorer by it. Therefore, expedients of this kind have the effect of increasing the distance which separates wealth from poverty, of paralyzing the social tendencies which are incessantly bringing men to the same level, and it will require centuries for the suffering classes to regain the ground which they have lost in their advance towards *equality of condition.**

---

* Although to all who have investigated the subject the evidence is conclusive that an irredeemable fluctuating paper money is always made an agency for taxing with special severity all that class of consumers who live on fixed incomes, salaries, and wages, it has, nevertheless, always been a somewhat difficult matter to find illustrations of the fact so clear and simple as to carry conviction by presentation that it does thus act to the classes most interested. With a view of obtaining such an illustration, application

B. Good morning; I shall go and meditate upon the lecture you have been giving me.

F. Have you finished your own dissertation? As for me, I have scarcely begun mine. I have not yet spoken of the popular *hatred* of capital, of gratuitous credit (loans without interest)—a most unfortunate notion, a deplorable mistake, which takes its rise from the same source.

B. What! does this frightful commotion of the populace against capitalists arise from money being confounded with wealth?

F. It is the result of different causes. Unfortunately, certain capitalists have arrogated to themselves monopolies and privileges which are quite sufficient to account for this feeling. But when the theorists of democracy have wished to justify it, to systematize it, to give it the appearance of a reasonable opinion, and to turn it against the very nature of capital, they have had

---

was made some some months since to an eminent American merchant (A. T. Stewart), whose large and varied experience abundantly qualified him to discuss the subject; and the result of the application may be thus stated:

Q. In buying in gold and selling in currency, what addition do you make to your selling price, in the way of insurance, that the currency received will be sufficient—plus profit, interest, etc.—to replace or buy back the gold represented by the original purchase?

recourse to that false political economy at whose root the same confusion is always to be found. They have said to the people:—" Take a dollar; put it under a glass; forget it for a year; then go and look at it, and you will be convinced that it has not produced ten cents, nor five cents, nor any

---

A. We do but very little of that now; hardly enough to speak about.

Q. But still you make insurance against currency fluctuations an item in your business to be regarded to some extent.

A. Why, yes, certainly; it won't do to overlook it entirely.

Q. Well, then, if you have no objections, please tell me what you do allow under existing circumstances?

A. I have certainly no objections. We buy closely for cash; sell largely for cash, or very short credit; and, within the comparatively narrow limits that currency has fluctuated for the last two or three years, add but little to our selling prices as insurance on that account, say one or two per cent. for cash, or three months' credit; and for a longer credit— if we give it—something additional. During or immediately after the war, when the currency fluctuations were more extensive, frequent, and capricious, the case was very different. Then selling prices had to be watched very closely, and changed very frequently, sometimes daily. My present experience, therefore, is exceptional; and to get the information you want, you must look further. I think I can help you to do this. We buy regularly large quantities of a foreign product, let us suppose, for illustration, *cloths*, for the large manufacturers and dealers in ready-made clothing. We buy for gold, and we sell for gold, and do not allow the fraction of a cent. Therefore, money produces no interest." Then, substituting for the word money, its pretended sign, *capital*, they have made it by their logic undergo this modification—" Then capital produces no interest." Then follows this series of consequences—" Therefore he

---

currency or its fluctuations to enter in any way into these transactions. But how is it with *my* customers? I allow them some credit; and the amount involved being often very large, I, of course, must know something of the way in which they manage their business. They transform the cloth purchased with gold into clothing, and then sell the clothing, in turn, to *their* customers, jobbers and retailers, all over the country, for currency, on a much longer average credit than they obtain from me for their raw material. As a matter of safety and necessity these wholesale dealers and manufacturers must add to their selling prices a sufficient percentage to make sure that the currency they are to receive at the end of three, six, or nine months will be sufficient to buy them as much gold as they have paid to me, or as much as will buy them another lot of cloth to meet the further demands of their business and their customers. How much they thus add I cannot definitely say. There is no regular rule. Every man doubtless adds all that competition will permit; and every circumstance likely to affect the prospective price of gold is carefully considered. Five per cent., in my opinion, on a credit of three months, would be the average minimum; and for a longer time, a larger percentage. If competition does not allow any insurance percentage to be added there is a liability to a loss of capital, which in the long run may be most disastrous, a circumstance that may explain the wreck of many firms, whose who lends a capital ought to obtain nothing from it; therefore he who lends you a capital, if he gains something by it, is robbing you; therefore all capitalists are robbers; therefore wealth, which ought to serve gratuitously those who borrow it, belongs in reality to those to whom it does not belong; therefore there is no such thing as property, therefore everything belongs to everybody; therefore . . . . "

---

managers, on the old-fashioned basis of doing business, would have been successful. The jobbers and the retailers, to whom the wholesale dealers and manufacturers sell, are not so likely to take currency insurance into consideration in fixing their selling prices; but to whatever amount the cost price of their goods has been enhanced by the necessity of insurance against currency fluctuations, on that same amount they estimate and add for interest and profits; the total enhancement of prices falling ultimately on the consumer, who, of necessity, can rarely know the elements of the cost of the article he purchases.

Q. So Mr. Webster, then, in his remark, which has become almost a proverb, that "of all contrivances for cheating the laboring classes, none has been more effectual than that which deludes them with paper money," must have been thoroughly cognizant of the nature of such transactions?

A. Most undoubtedly; for such transactions are the inevitable consequence of using as a medium of exchange a variable, irredeemable currency.

The illustration above given, therefore, in the place of being imaginary, is based on the actual condition of business at the present time, January, 1876.—*Note from Robinson Crusoe's Money*, by David A. Wells.

B. This is very serious; the more so, from the syllogism being so admirably formed. I should very much like to be enlightened on the subject. But, alas! I can no longer command my attention. There is such a confusion in my head of the words *coin, money, services, capital, interest,* that really I hardly know where I am. We will, if you please, resume the conversation another day.

F. In the meantime here is a little work entitled *Capital and Rent.* It may perhaps remove some of your doubts. Just look at it when you are in want of a little amusement.

B. To amuse me?

F. Who knows? One nail drives in another; one wearisome thing drives away another.

B. I have not yet made up my mind that your views upon money and political economy in general are correct. But, from your conversation, this is what I have gathered:—That these questions are of the highest importance; for peace or war, order or anarchy, the union or the antagonism of citizens, are at the root of the answer to them. How is it that in France and most other countries which regard themselves as highly civilized, a science which concerns us all so nearly, and the diffusion of which would have so decisive an influence upon the fate of mankind, is so little known? Is it that the State does not teach it sufficiently?

F. Not exactly. For, without knowing it, the State applies itself to loading everybody's brain with prejudices, and everybody's heart with sentiments favorable to the spirit of anarchy, war, and hatred; so that, when a doctrine of order, peace, and union presents itself, it is in vain that it has clearness and truth on its side,—it cannot gain admittance.

B. Decidedly you are a frightful grumbler. What interest can the State have in mystifying people's intellects in favor of revolutions, and civil and foreign wars? There must certainly be a great deal of exaggeration in what you say.

F. Consider. At the period when our intellectual faculties begin to develop themselves, at the age when impressions are liveliest, when habits of mind are formed with the greatest ease—when we might look at society and understand it—in a word, as soon as we are seven or eight years old, what does the State do? It puts a bandage over our eyes, takes us gently from the midst of the social circle which surrounds us, to plunge us, with our susceptible faculties, our impressible hearts, into the midst of Roman society. It keeps us there for ten years at least, long enough to make an ineffaceable impression on the brain. Now observe, that Roman society is directly opposed to what our society ought to be. There they lived upon war; here we ought to hate war; there they hated labor; here we ought to live upon labor. There the means of subsistence were founded upon slavery and plunder; here they should be drawn from free industry. Roman society was organized in consequence of its principle. It necessarily admired what made it prosper. There they considered as virtue what we look upon as vice. Its poets and historians had to exalt what we ought to despise. The very words *liberty, order, justice, people, honor, influence, etc.*, could not have the same signification at Rome, as they have, or ought to have, at Paris. How can you expect that all these youths who have been at university or conventual schools, with Livy and Quintus Curtius for their catechism, will not understand liberty like the Gracchi, virtue like Cato, patriotism like Cæsar? How can you expect them not to be factious and warlike? How can you expect them to take the slightest interest in the mechanism of our social order? Do you think that their minds have been prepared to understand it? Do you not see that in order to do so they must get rid of their present impressions, and receive others entirely opposed to them?

B. What do you conclude from that?

F. I will tell you. The most urgent necessity is, not that the State should teach, but that it should *allow* education. All monopolies are detestable, but the worst of all is the monopoly of education.

THE LAW.

The law perverted! The law—and, in its wake, all the collective forces of the nation—the law, I say, not only diverted from its proper direction, but made to pursue one entirely contrary! The law become the tool of every kind of avarice, instead of being its check! The law guilty of that very iniquity which it was its mission to punish! Truly, this is a serious fact, if it exists, and one to which I feel bound to call the attention of my fellow-citizens.

We hold from God the gift which, as far as we are concerned, contains all others, Life—physical, intellectual, and moral life.

But life cannot support itself. He who has bestowed it, has entrusted us with the care of supporting it, of developing it, and of perfecting it. To that end He has provided us with a collection of wonderful faculties; He has plunged us into the midst of a variety of elements. It is by the application of our faculties to these elements that the phenomena of assimilation and of appropriation, by which life pursues the circle which has been assigned to it, are realized.

Existence, faculties, assimilation — in other words, personality, liberty, property—this is man. It is of these three things that it may be said, apart from all demagogue subtlety, that they are anterior and superior to all human legislation.

It is not because men have made laws, that personality, liberty, and property exist. On the contrary, it is because personality, liberty, and property exist beforehand, that men make laws.

What, then, is law? As I have said elsewhere, it is the collective organization of the individual right to lawful defense.

Nature, or rather God, has bestowed upon every one of us the right to defend his person, his liberty, and his property, since these are the three constituent or preserving elements of life; elements, each of which is rendered complete by the others, and cannot be understood without them. For what are our faculties but the extension of our personality? and what is property but an extension of our faculties?

If every man has the right of defending, even by force, his person, his liberty, and his property, a number of men have the right to combine together, to extend, to organize a common force, to provide regularly for this defense.

Collective right, then, has its principle, its reason for existing, its lawfulness, in individual right; and the common force cannot rationally have any other end, or any other mission, than that of the isolated forces for which it is substituted. Thus, as the force of an individual cannot lawfully touch the person, the liberty, or the property of another individual—for the same reason, the common force cannot lawfully be used to destroy the person, the liberty, or the property of individuals or of classes.

For this perversion of force would be, in one case as in the other, in contradiction to our premises. For who will assume to say that force has been given to us, not to defend our rights, but to annihilate the equal rights of our brethren? And if this be not true of every individual force, acting independently, how can it be true of the collective force, which is only the organized union of isolated forces?

Nothing, therefore, can be more evident than this:—The law is the organization of the natural right of lawful defense; it is the substitution of collective for individual forces, for the purpose of acting in the sphere in which such collective forces have a right to act, of doing what they have a right to do, to secure persons, liberties, and properties, and to maintain each in its right, so as to cause justice to reign over all.

And if a people established upon this basis were to exist, it seems to me that order would prevail among them in their acts as well as in their ideas. It seems to me that such a people would have the most simple, the most economical, the least oppressive, the least to be felt, the least responsible, the most just, and, consequently, the most solid Government which could be imagined, whatever its political form might be.

For, under such an administration, every one would feel that he possessed all the fullness, as well as all the responsibility of his existence. So long as personal safety was insured, so long as labor was free, and the fruits of labor secured against all unjust attacks, no one would have any difficulties to contend with in the State. When prosperous, we should not, it is true, have to thank the State for our success; but when unfortunate, we should no more think of taxing it with our disasters than our peasants think of attributing to it the arrival of hail or of frost. We should know it only by the inestimable blessing of Safety.

It may further be affirmed, that, thanks to the non-intervention of the State in private affairs, our wants and their satisfactions would develop themselves in their natural order. We should not see poor families seeking for literary instruction before they were supplied with bread. We should not see towns peopled at the expense of rural districts, nor rural districts at the expense of towns. We should not see those great displacements of capital, of labor, and of population, which legislative measures occasion; displacements which render so uncertain and precarious the very sources of existence, and thus aggravate to such an extent the responsibility of Governments.

Unhappily law is by no means confined to its own department. Nor is it merely in some indifferent and debatable views that it has left its proper sphere. It has done more than this. It has acted in direct opposition to its proper end; it has destroyed its own object; it has been employed in annihilating that justice which it ought to have established, in effacing among Rights that limit which was its true mission to respect; it has placed the collective force in the service of those who wish to traffic, without risk and without scruple, in the persons, the liberty, and the property of others; it has converted plunder into a right, that it may protect it, and lawful defense into a crime, that it may punish it.

How has this perversion of law been accomplished? And what has resulted from it?

The law has been perverted through the influence of two very different causes—bare egotism and false philanthropy.

Let us speak of the former.

Self-preservation and developement is the common aspiration of all men, in such a way that if every one enjoyed the free exercise of his faculties and the free disposition of the fruits of their labor, social progress would be incessant, uninterrupted, inevitable.

But there is also another disposition which is common to them. This is, to live and to develop, when they can, at the expense of one another. This is no rash imputation, emanating from a gloomy, uncharitable spirit. History bears witness to the truth of it, by the incessant wars, the migrations of races, sacerdotal oppressions, the universality of slavery, the frauds in trade, and the monopolies with which its annals abound. This unfortunate disposition has its origin in the very constitution of man—in that primitive, and universal, and invincible sentiment which urges it towards its well-being, and makes it seek to escape pain.

Man can only maintain life and obtain enjoyment from a perpetual search and appropriation; that is, from a perpetual application of his faculties to objects, or from labor. This is the origin of property.

But yet he may live and enjoy, by seizing, and appropriating the productions of his fellow-men. This is the origin of plunder.

Now, labor being in itself a pain, and man being

naturally inclined to avoid pain, it follows, and history proves it, that wherever plunder is less burdensome than labor, it prevails; and neither religion nor morality can, in this case, prevent it from prevailing.

When does plunder cease, then? When it becomes more difficult and more dangerous than labor. It is very evident that the proper aim of law is to oppose the powerful obstacle of collective force to the tendency to do wrong; that all its measures should be in favor of the security of property, and against plunder.

But the law is made, generally, by one man, or by one class of men. And as law cannot exist without the sanction and the support of a preponderating force, it must finally place this force in the hands of those who legislate.

This inevitable phenomenon, combined with the fatal tendency which, we have said, exists in the heart of man, explains the almost universal perversion of law. It is easy to conceive that, instead of being a check upon injustice, it becomes its most invincible instrument. It is easy to conceive that, according to the power of the legislator, it destroys for its own profit, and in different degrees, amongst the rest of the community, personal independence by slavery, liberty by oppression, and property by plunder.

It is in the nature of men to rise against the injustice of which they are the victims. When, therefore, plunder is organized by law, for the profit of those who perpetrate it, all the plundered classes tend, either by peaceful or revolutionary means, to enter in some way into the business of manufacturing laws. These classes, according to the degree of enlightenment at which they have arrived, may propose to themselves two very different ends, when they thus attempt the attainment of their political rights; either they may wish to put an end to lawful plunder, or they may desire to take part in it.

Woe to the nation where this latter thought prevails amongst the masses, at the moment when they, in their turn, seize upon the legislative power!

Up to that time lawful plunder has been exercised by the few upon the many, as is the case in countries where the right of legislating is confined to a few hands. But now it has become universal, and the equilibrium is sought in universal plunder. The injustice which society contains, instead of being rooted out of it, is generalized. As soon as the injured classes have recovered their political rights, their first thought is not to abolish plunder (this would suppose them to possess enlightenment, which they cannot have), but to organize against the other classes, and to their detriment, a system of reprisals—as if it was necessary, before the reign of justice arrives, that all should undergo a cruel retribution—some for their iniquity and some for their ignorance.

It would be impossible, therefore, to introduce into society a greater change and a greater evil than this—the conversion of the law into an instrument of plunder.

What would be the consequences of such a perversion? It would require volumes to describe them all. We must content ourselves with pointing out the most striking.

In the first place, it would efface from everybody's conscience the distinction between justice and injustice.

No society can exist unless the laws are respected to a certain degree, but the safest way to make them respected is to make them respectable. When law and morality are in contradiction to each other, the citizen finds himself in the cruel alternative of either losing his moral sense, or of losing his respect for the law—two evils of equal magnitude, between which it would be difficult to choose.

It is so much in the nature of law to support justice, that in the minds of the masses they are one and the same. There is in all of us a strong disposition to regard what is lawful as legitimate, so much so, that many falsely derive all notions of justice from law. It is sufficient, then, for the law to order and sanction plunder, that it may appear to many consciences just and sacred. Slavery, protection, and monopoly find defenders, not only in those who profit by them, but in those who suffer by them. If you suggest a doubt as to the morality of these institutions, it is said directly—"You are a dangerous innovator, a utopian, a theorist, a despiser of the laws; you would shake the basis upon which society rests."

If you lecture upon morality, or political economy, somebody will be found to make this request to the proper authorities :—

"That henceforth economic science be taught not only with sole reference to free exchange (to liberty, property, and justice), as has been the case up to the present time, but also, and especially with reference to the facts and legislation (contrary to liberty, property, and justice) which regulate domestic industry.

"That in public pulpits the preachers abstain rigorously from impairing in the slightest degree the respect due to the laws now in force." *

---

* Proceedings of the French General Council of Manufactures, Agriculture, and Commerce, 6th of May, 1850.

So that if a law exists which sanctions slavery or monopoly, oppression or plunder, in any form whatever, it must not even be mentioned—for how can it be mentioned without damaging the respect which it inspires? Still further, morality and political economy must be taught in connection with this law—that is, under the supposition that it must be just, only because it is law.

Another effect of this deplorable perversion of the law is, that it gives to human passions and to political struggles, and in general to politics, properly so called, an exaggerated preponderance.

I could prove this assertion in a thousand ways. But I shall confine myself, by way of illustration, to bringing it to bear upon a subject which has of late occupied everybody's mind—universal suffrage.

Whatever may be thought of it, I maintain that *universal* suffrage (taking the word in its strictest sense) is not one of those sacred dogmas with respect to which examination and doubt are crimes.

Serious objections may be made to it.

In the first place, the word *universal* conceals a gross sophism. There are, in France, for example, 36,000,000 of inhabitants. To make the right of suffrage universal, 36,000,000 of electors should be reckoned. The most extended system reckons only 9,000,000. Three persons out of four, then, are excluded; and more than this, they are excluded by the fourth. Upon what principle is this exclusion founded? Upon the principle of incapacity. Universal suffrage, then, means—universal suffrage of those who are capable. In point of fact, who are the capable? Are age, sex, and judicial condemnations the only conditions to which incapacity is to be attached?

On taking a nearer view of the subject, we may soon perceive the motive which causes the right of suffrage to depend upon the presumption of incapacity; the most extended system differing only in this respect from the most restricted, by the appreciation of those conditions on which this incapacity depends, and which constitute, not a difference in principle but in degree.

This motive is, that the elector does not stipulate for himself, but for everybody.

If, as the republicans of the Greek and Roman tone pretend, the right of suffrage had fallen to the lot of every one at his birth, it would be an injustice to adults to prevent women and children from voting. Why are they prevented? Because they are presumed to be incapable. And why is incapacity a motive for exclusion? Because the elector does not alone sustain the responsibility of his vote; because every vote affects the community at large; because the community has a right to demand some security of each elector in respect to the performance of acts upon which his well-being depends.

I know what might be said in answer to this, I know what might be objected. But this is not the place to enter into a controversy of this kind. What I wish to observe is this, that this same controversy about suffrage (in common with most political questions) which agitates, excites, and unsettles the nations, would lose almost all its importance if the law had always been what it ought to be.

In fact, if law were confined to causing all persons, all liberties, and all properties to be respected; if it were merely the organization of individual right and individual defense; if it were the obstacle, the check, the chastisement opposed to all oppression, to all plunder—is it likely that we should dispute much, as citizens, on the subject of the greater or less universality of suffrage? Is it likely that such disputes would compromise that greatest of advantages, the public peace? Is it likely that the excluded classes would not quietly wait for their political recognition? Is it likely that the enfranchised classes would be very jealous of their privilege? And is it not clear, that the interest of all being one and the same, a few would manage political affairs without much inconvenience to the others?

But if the fatal principle should come to be introduced, that, under pretense of organization, regulation, protection, or encouragement, the law may take from one party in order to give to another; help itself to wealth acquired by all classes that it may increase that of one class, whether that of the agriculturists, the manufacturers, the shipowners, or artists and comedians; then certainly, in this case, there is no class which may not pretend, and with reason, to place its hand upon the law; which would not demand with fury its right of election and eligibility, and which would not overturn society rather than not obtain it. Even beggars and vagabonds will prove to you that they have an incontestable title to suffrage. They will say—" We never buy wine, tobacco, or salt, without paying the tax, and a part of this tax is given by law in perquisites and gratuities to men who are richer than we are. Others make use of the law to create an artificial rise in the price of bread, meat, iron, or cloth. Since everybody traffics in law for his own profit, we should like to do the same. We should like to make it affirm the *right to assistance*, public and private, which is the poor man's plunder. To effect this, we ought to be electors and legislators, that we may organize, on a large scale, alms for our own class, as you have organized, on a large scale, protection for yours. Don't tell us that you will take our cause upon yourselves, and throw to us bounties and offices to keep us quiet, like giving us a bone to pick. We have other claims, and, at any rate, we wish to stipulate for ourselves, as other classes have stipulated for themselves!" How is this argument to be answered? Yes, as long as it is admitted that the law may be diverted from its true mission, that it may violate property instead of securing it, everybody will be wanting to manufacture law, either to defend himself against plunder, or to organize it for his own profit. The political question will always be prejudicial, predominant, and absorbing; in a word, there will be fighting around the door of the Legislative Chambers. The struggle will be no less furious within them. To be convinced of this, it is hardly necessary to look at what passes in the Chambers in France, in England, and in the United States; it is enough to know how the question stands.

Is there any need to prove that this odious perversion of law is a perpetual source of hatred and discord—that it even tends to social disorganization? Look at the United States. There is no country in the world where the law is kept more within its proper domain—which is, to secure to every one his liberty and his property. Therefore, there is no country in the world where social order *appears* to rest upon a more solid basis. Nevertheless, even in the United States, there are two questions, and only two, which from the beginning have endangered political order. And what are these two questions? That of slavery and that of the tariff;* that is, precisely the only two questions in which, contrary to the general spirit of this republic, law has taken the character of a plunderer. Slavery is a violation, sanctioned by law, of the rights of the person. Protection is a violation perpetrated by the law upon the rights of property; and certainly it is very remarkable that, in the midst of so many other debates, this double *legal scourge*, a sorrowful inheritance from the Old World, should be the only one which can, and perhaps will, cause the rupture of the Union. Indeed, a more astounding fact, in the heart of society, cannot be conceived than this:—That *law should have become an instrument of injustice.* And if this fact occasions consequences so formidable to the United States, where there is but one exception, what must it be with us in Europe, where it is a principle—a system?

M. Montalembert, adopting the thought of a

---

* The reader will bear in mind that this essay was written by M. Bastiat before the emancipation in the United States.

famous proclamation of M. Carlier, said, "We must make war against socialism." And by socialism, according to the definition of M. Charles Dupin, he meant plunder.

But what plunder did he mean? For there are two sorts—*extra-legal* and *legal plunder*.

As to extra-legal plunder, such as theft, or swindling, which is defined, foreseen, and punished by the penal code, I do not think it can be adorned by the name of socialism. It is not this which systematically threatens the foundations of society. Besides, the war against this kind of plunder has not waited for the signal of M. Montalembert or M. Carlier. It has gone on since the beginning of the world; France was carrying it on long before the revolution of February, 1848 —long before the appearance of socialism—with all the ceremonies of magistracy, police, prisons, dungeons, and scaffolds. It is the law itself which is conducting this war, and it is to be wished, in my opinion, that the law should always maintain this attitude with respect to plunder.

But this is not the case. The law sometimes takes its own part. Sometimes it accomplishes it with its own hands, in order to save the parties benefited the shame, the danger, and the scruple. Sometimes it places all this ceremony of magistracy, police, gendarmerie, and prisons, at the service of the plunderer, and treats the plundered party, when he defends himself, as the criminal. In a word, there is a *legal plunder*, and it is, no doubt, this which is meant by M. Montalembert.

This plunder may be only an exceptional blemish in the legislation of a people, and in this case the best thing that can be done is, without so many speeches and lamentations, to do away with it as soon as possible, notwithstanding the clamors of interested parties. But how is it to be distinguished? Very easily. See whether the law takes from some persons that which belongs to them, to give to others what does not belong to them. See whether the law performs, for the profit of one citizen, and to the injury of others, an act which this citizen cannot perform without committing a crime. Abolish this law without delay; it is not merely an iniquity—it is a fertile source of iniquities, for it invites reprisals; and if you do not take care, the exceptional case will extend, multiply, and become systematic. No doubt the party benefited will protest loudly; he will assert his *acquired rights*. He will say that the State is bound to protect and encourage his industry; he will plead that it is a good thing for the State to be enriched, that it may spend the more, and thus shower down salaries upon the poor workmen. Take care not to listen to this sophistry, for it is just by the generalizing of these arguments that legal-plunder becomes systematized.

And this is what has taken place. The delusion of the day is to enrich all classes at the expense of each other; it is to generalize plunder under pretense of organizing it. Now, legal plunder may be exercised in an infinite multitude of ways. Hence come an infinite multitude of plans for organization; tariffs, protection, perquisites, gratuities, encouragements, progressive taxation, gratuitous instruction, right to labor, right to profit, right to wages, right to assistance, right to instruments of labor, gratuity of credit, etc., etc. And it is all these plans, taken as a whole, with what they have in common, legal plunder, which takes the name of socialism.

Now socialism, thus defined, and forming a doctrinal body, what other war would you make against it than a war of doctrine? You find this doctrine false, absurd, abominable. Refute it. This will be all the more easy, the more false, the more absurd and the more abominable it is. Above all, if you wish to be strong, begin by rooting out of your legislation every particle of socialism which may have crept into it,—and this will be no light work.

M. Montalembert has been reproached with

wishing to turn brute force against socialism. He ought to be exonerated from this reproach, for he has plainly said:—"The war which we must make against socialism must be one which is compatible with the law, honor, and justice."

But how is it that M. Montalembert does not see that he is placing himself in a vicious circle? You would oppose law to socialism. But it is the law which socialism invokes. It aspires to legal, not extra-legal plunder. It is the law itself, in common with monopolists of all kinds, that socialism wants to use as an instrument; and when once it has the law on its side, how will you be able to turn the law against it? How will you place it under the power of your tribunals, your police, and of your prisons? What will you do then? You wish to prevent it from taking any part in the making of laws. You would keep it outside the Legislative Halls. In this you will not succeed, I venture to prophesy, so long as legal plunder is the basis of the legislation within.

It is absolutely necessary that this question of legal plunder should be clearly defined, and there are only three solutions of it:—

1. When the few plunder the many.
2. When everybody plunders everybody else.
3. When nobody plunders anybody.

Partial plunder, universal plunder, absence of plunder, amongst these we have to make our choice. The law can only produce one of these results.

Partial plunder.—This is the system which prevailed so long as the elective privilege was *partial*—a system which is resorted to to avoid the invasion of socialism.

Universal plunder.—We have been threatened by this system when the elective privilege has become universal; the masses having conceived the idea of making law on the principle of legislators who had preceded them.

Absence of plunder.—This is the principle of justice, peace, order, stability, conciliation, and of good sense, which I shall proclaim with all the force of my lungs (which is very inadequate, alas!) till the day of my death.

And, in all sincerity, can anything more be required at the hands of the law? Can the law, whose necessary sanction is force, be reasonably employed upon anything beyond securing to every one his right? I defy any one to remove it from this circle without perverting it, and consequently turning force against right. And as this is the most fatal, the most illogical social perversion which can possibly be imagined, it must be admitted that the true solution, so much sought after, of the social problem, is contained in these simple words—LAW IS ORGANIZED JUSTICE.

Now it is important to remark, that to organize justice by law, that is to say by force, excludes the idea of organizing by law, or by force any manifestation whatever of human activity—labor, charity, agriculture, commerce, industry, instruction, the fine arts, or religion; for any one of these organizations would inevitably destroy the essential organization. How, in fact, can we imagine force encroaching upon the liberty of citizens without infringing upon justice, and so acting against its proper aim?

Here I am encountering the most popular prejudice of our time. It is not considered enough that law should be just, it must be philanthropic. It is not sufficient that it should guarantee to every citizen the free and inoffensive exercise of his faculties, applied to his physical, intellectual, and moral development; it is required to extend well-being, instruction, and morality, directly over the nation. This is the fascinating side of socialism.

But, I repeat it, these two missions of the law contradict each other. We have to choose between them. A citizen cannot at the same time be free and not free. M. de Lamartine wrote to me one day thus:—" Your doctrine is only the half of my programme; you have stopped at liberty, I go on to fraternity." I answered him:—" The second part of your programme will destroy the first." And in fact it is impossible for me to separate the word *fraternity* from the world *voluntary*. I cannot possibly conceive fraternity as something which has got to be *legally* enforced, without liberty being *legally* destroyed, and justice *legally* trampled under foot. Legal plunder has two roots: one of them, as we have already seen, is in human selfishness; the other is in false philanthropy.

Before I proceed I think I ought to explain myself upon the word plunder.*

I do not take it, as it often is taken, in a vague, undefined, relative, or metaphorical sense. I use it in its scientific acceptation, and as expressing the opposite idea to property. When a portion of wealth passes out of the hands of him who has acquired it, without his consent, and without compensation, to him who has not created it, whether by force or by artifice, I say that property is violated, that plunder is perpetrated. I say that this is exactly what the law ought to repress always and everywhere. If the law itself performs the action it ought to repress, I say that plunder is

---

* The French word is *spoliation*.

still perpetrated, and even, in a social point of view, under aggravated circumstances. In this case, however, he who profits from the plunder is not responsible for it; it is the law, the lawgiver, society itself, and this is where the political danger lies.

It is to be regretted that there is something offensive in the word. I have sought in vain for another, for I would not wish at any time to add an irritating word to our dissensions; therefore, whether I am believed or not, I declare that I do not mean to accuse the intentions nor the morality of anybody. I am attacking an idea which I believe to be false—a system which appears to me to be unjust; and this is so independent of intentions that each of us profits by it without wishing it, and suffers from it without being aware of the cause. Any person must write under the influence of party spirit or of fear who would call in question the sincerity of the advocates of protectionism, of socialism, and even of communism, which are one and the same plant, in three different periods of its growth. All that can be said is, that plunder is more visible by its partiality in protectionism,* and by its universality in communism;

---

* If protection were only granted in a country—as, for example, the United States—to a single class, to the cotton-manufactures, for instance, it would be so obviously plun-

whence it follows that, of the three systems, socialism is still the most vague, the most undefined, and consequently the most sincere.

Be it as it may, to conclude that legal plunder has one of its roots in false philanthropy, is evidently to put intentions out of the question.

With this understanding, let us examine the value, the origin, and the tendency of this popular aspiration, which pretends to realize the general good by general plunder.

The Socialists say, since the law organizes justice, why should it not organize labor, instruction, and religion?

Why? Because it could not organize labor, instruction, and religion, without disorganizing justice.

For remember that law is force, and that consequently the domain of the law cannot lawfully extend beyond the domain of force.

When law and force keep a man within the bounds of justice, they impose nothing upon him but a mere negation. They only oblige him to

---

dering as to be unable to maintain itself. But the fact is, all the protected trades combine, make common cause, and recruit themselves in such a way as to make it appear as if they included in their sphere the whole industry of the country. They feel instinctively that plunder is disguised by being generalized.

abstain from doing harm. They violate neither his personality, his liberty, nor his property. They only guard the personality, the liberty, the property of others. They hold themselves on the defensive; they defend the equal right of all. They fulfill a mission whose harmlessness is evident, whose utility is palpable, and whose legitimacy is not to be disputed. This is so true that, as a friend of mine once remarked to me, to say that *the aim of the law is to cause justice to reign*, is to use an expression which is not rigorously exact. It ought to be said, *the aim of the law is to prevent injustice from reigning*. In fact, it is not justice which has an existence of its own, it is injustice. The one results from the absence of the other.

But when the law, through the medium of its necessary agent—force, imposes a form of labor, a method or a subject of instruction, a creed or a worship, it is no longer negative; it acts positively upon men. It substitutes the will of the legislator for their own will, the initiative of the legislator for their own initiative. They have no need to consult, to compare, or to foresee; the law does all that for them. The intellect is for them a useless lumber; they cease to be men; they lose their personality, their liberty their property.

Endeavor to imagine a form of labor imposed by force which is not a violation of liberty; a transmission of wealth imposed by force which is not a violation of property. If you cannot succeed in reconciling this, you are bound to conclude that the law cannot organize labor and industry without organizing injustice.

When, from the seclusion of his cabinet, a politician takes a view of society, he is struck with the spectacle of inequality which presents itself. He mourns over the sufferings which are the lot of so many of our brethren, sufferings whose aspect is rendered yet more sorrowful by the contrast of luxury and wealth.

He ought, perhaps, to ask himself whether such a social state has not been caused by the plunder of ancient times, exercised in the way of conquests; and by plunder of later times, effected through the medium of the laws? He ought to ask himself whether, granting the aspiration of all men after well-being and perfection, the reign of justice would not suffice to realize the greatest activity of progress, and the greatest amount of equality compatible with that individual responsibility which God has awarded as a just retribution of virtue and vice ?

He never gives this a thought. His mind turns toward combinations, arrangements, legal or factitious organizations. He seeks the remedy in perpetuating and exaggerating what has produced the evil.

For, justice apart, which we have seen is only a negation, is there any one of these legal arrangements which does not contain the principle of plunder?

You say, "There are men who have no money," and you apply to the law. But the law is not a self-supplied fountain, whence every stream may obtain supplies independently of society. Nothing can enter the public treasury, in favor of one citizen or one class, but what other citizens and other classes have been *forced* to send to it. If every one draws from it only the equivalent of what he has contributed to it, your law, it is true, is no plunderer, but it does nothing for men who want money—it does not promote equality. It can only be an instrument of equalization as far as it takes from one party to give to another, and then it is an instrument of plunder. Examine, in this light, the protection of tariffs, prizes for encouragement, right to profit, right to labor, right to assistance, right to instruction, progressive taxation, gratuitousness of credit, social workshops, and you will always find at the bottom legal plunder, organized injustice.

You say, "There are men who want knowledge," and you apply to the law. But the law is not a torch which sheds light abroad which is peculiar to itself. It extends over a society where there are men who have knowledge, and others who have not; citizens who want to learn, and others who are disposed to teach. It can only do one of two things: either allow a free scope to this kind of transaction, *i.e.*, let this kind of want satisfy itself freely; or else force the will of the people in the matter, and take from some of them sufficient to pay professors commissioned to instruct others gratuitously. But, in this second case, there cannot fail to be a violation of liberty and property—legal plunder.

You say, "Here are men who are wanting in morality or religion;" and you apply to the law; but law is force, and need I say how far it is a violent and absurd enterprise to introduce force in these matters?

As the result of its systems and of its efforts, it would seem that socialism, notwithstanding all its self-complacency, can scarcely help perceiving the monster of legal plunder. But what does it do? It disguises it cleverly from others, and even from itself, under the seductive names of fraternity, solidarity, organization, association. And because we do not ask so much at the hands of the law, because we only ask it for justice, it supposes that we reject fraternity, solidarity, organization, and association; and they brand us with the name of *individualists*.

We can assure them that what we repudiate is, not natural organization, but forced organization.

It is not free association, but the forms of association which they would impose upon us.

It is not spontaneous fraternity, but legal fraternity.

It is not providential solidarity, but artificial solidarity, which is only an unjust displacement of responsibility.

Socialism, like the old policy from which it emanates, confounds Government and society. And so, every time we object to a thing being done by Government, it concludes that we object to its being done at all. We disapprove of education by the State—then we are against education altogether. We object to a State religion—then we would have no religion at all. We object to an equality which is brought about by the State—then we are against equality etc., etc. They might as well accuse us of wishing men not to eat, because we object to the cultivation of corn by the State.

How is it that the strange idea of making the law produce what it does not contain—prosperity, in a positive sense, wealth, science, religion—should ever have gained ground in the political world? The modern politicians, particularly those of the Socialist school, found their different theories upon one common hypothesis; and surely a more strange, a more presumptuous notion, could never have entered a human brain.

They divide mankind into two parts. Men in general, except one, form the first; the politician himself forms the second, which is by far the most important.

In fact, they begin by supposing that men are devoid of any principle of action, and of any means of discernment in themselves; that they have no moving spring in them; that they are inert matter, passive particles, atoms without impulse; at best a vegetation indifferent to its own mode of existence, susceptible of receiving, from an exterior will and hand, an infinite number of forms, more or less symmetrical, artistic, and perfected.

Moreover, every one of these politicians does not scruple to imagine that he himself is, under the names of organizer, discoverer, legislator, institutor or founder, this will and hand, this universal spring, this creative power, whose sublime mission it is to gather together these scattered materials, that is, men into society.

Starting from these data, as a gardener, according to his caprice, shapes his trees into pyramids, parasols, cubes, cones, vases, distaffs, or fans; so the Socialist, following his chimera, shapes poor humanity into groups, series, circles, subcircles, honeycombs, or social workshops, with all kinds of variations. And as the gardener, to bring his trees into shape, wants hatchets, pruning-hooks, saws, and shears, so the politician, to bring society into shape, wants the forces which he can only find in the laws; the law of customs, the law of taxation, the law of assistance, and the law of instruction.

It is so true that the Socialists look upon mankind as a subject for social combinations, that if, by chance, they are not quite certain of the success of these combinations, they will request a portion of mankind as a subject to experiment upon. It is well known how popular the idea of *trying all systems* is, and one of the French Socialists once seriously demanded of the French Constituent Assembly a parish, with all its inhabitants, upon which to make his experiments.

It is thus that an inventor will make a small machine before he makes one of the regular size. Thus the chemist sacrifices some substances, the agriculturist some seed and a corner of his field, to make trial of an idea.

But, then, think of the immeasurable distance between the gardener and his trees, between the inventor and his machine, between the chemist and his substances, between the agriculturist and his seed! The Socialist thinks, in all sincerity, that there is the same distance between himself and mankind.

It is not to be wondered at that the politicians of the nineteenth century look upon society as an artificial production of the legislator's genius. This idea has taken possession of many thinkers and great writers in all countries.

To all these persons the relations between mankind and the legislator appear to be the same as those which exist between the clay and the potter.

Moreover, if they have consented to recognize in the heart of man a principle of action, and in his intellect a principle of discernment, they have looked upon these gifts of God as pernicious, and thought that mankind, under these two impulses, tended fatally toward ruin. They have taken it for granted that, if abandoned to their own inclinations, men would only occupy themselves with religion to arrive at atheism, with instruction to come to ignorance, and with labor and exchange to be extinguished in misery.

Happily, according to these writers, there are some men, termed governors and legislators, upon whom Heaven has bestowed opposite tendencies, not for their own sake only, but for the sake of the rest of the world.

Whilst mankind tends to evil, they incline to good; whilst mankind is advancing toward darkness, they are aspiring to enlightenment; whilst mankind is drawn toward vice, they are attracted by virtue. And, this granted, they demand the assistance of force, by means of which they are to substitute their own tendencies for those of the human race.

It is only needful to open, almost at random, a book on philosophy, politics, or history, to see how strongly this idea is rooted in literature; that mankind is merely inert matter, receiving life, organization, morality, and wealth from power; or, rather, and still worse—that mankind itself tends toward degradation, and is only arrested in its tendency by the mysterious hand of the legislator. Classical conventionalism shows us everywhere, behind passive society, a hidden power, under the names of Law, or Legislator (or, by a mode of expression which refers to some person or persons of undisputed weight and authority, but not named), which moves, animates, enriches, and regenerates mankind.

We will first ask attention to a quotation from Bossuet:—

"One of the things which was the most strongly impressed (by whom?) upon the mind of the Egyptians, was the love of their country. . . . . *Nobody was allowed* to be useless to the State; the law assigned to every one his employment, which descended from father to son. No one was permitted to have two professions, nor to adopt another.

..... But there was one occupation which *was obliged* to be common to all—this was the study of the laws and of wisdom; ignorance of religion and the political regulations of the country was excused in no condition of life. Moreover, every profession had a district assigned to it (by whom ?).
..... Amongst good laws, one of the best things was that everybody was taught to observe them (by whom ?). Egypt abounded with wonderful inventions, and nothing was neglected which could render life comfortable and tranquil."

Thus men, according to Bossuet, derive nothing from themselves; patriotism, wealth, inventions, husbandry, science—all come to them by the operation of the laws, or by kings. All they have to do is to be passive. It is on this ground that Bossuet takes exception, when Diodorus accuses the Egyptians of rejecting wrestling and music. "How is that possible," says he, "since these arts were invented by Trismegistus?"

It is the same with the Persians:—

"One of the first cares of the prince was to encourage agriculture. ..... As there were posts established for the regulation of the armies, so there were offices for the superintending of rural works. ..... The respect with which the Persians were inspired for royal authority was excessive."

The Greeks, although full of mind, were no less strangers to their own responsibilities; so much so, that of themselves, like dogs and horses, they would not have ventured upon the most simple games. In a classical sense, it is an undisputed thing that everything comes to the people from without.

"The Greeks, naturally full of spirit and courage, *had been early cultivated* by kings and colonies who had come from Egypt. From them they had learned the exercises of the body, *foot races*, and horse and chariot races. . . . . The best thing that the Egyptians had taught them was to become docile, and to allow themselves to be formed by the laws for the public good."

Fénelon.—Reared in the study and admiration of antiquity, and a witness of the power of Louis XIV., Fénelon naturally adopted the idea that mankind should be passive, and that its misfortunes and its prosperities, its virtues and its vices, are caused by the external influence which is exercised upon it by the *law*, or by the makers of the law. Thus, in his Utopia of Salentum, he brings the men, with their interests, their faculties, their desires, and their possessions, under the absolute direction of the legislator. Whatever the subject may be, they themselves have no voice in it—the prince judges for them. The nation is just a shapeless mass, of which the prince is the soul. In him resides the thought, the foresight, the principle of all organization, of all progress; on him, therefore, rests all the responsibility.

In proof of this assertion, I might transcribe the whole of the tenth book of "Telemachus."

I refer the reader to it, and shall content myself with quoting some passages taken at random from this celebrated work, to which, in every other respect, I am most ready to render justice.

With the astonishing credulity which characterizes the classics, Fénelon, against the authority of reason and of facts, admits the general felicity of the Egyptians, and attributes it, not to their own wisdom, but to that of their kings:—

"We could not turn our eyes to the two shores without perceiving rich towns and country seats, agreeably situated; fields which were covered every year, without intermission, with golden crops; meadows full of flocks; laborers bending under the weight of fruits which the earth lavished on its cultivators; and shepherds who made the echoes around repeat the soft sounds of their pipes and flutes. 'Happy,' said Mentor, 'is that people which is governed by a wise king. . . . . . Mentor afterwards desired me to remark the happiness and abundance which was spread over all the country of Egypt, where twenty-two thousand cities might be counted. He admired the excellent police regulations of the cities; the justice administered in favor of the poor *against* the rich; the good education of the children, who were accustomed to obedience, labor, and the love of arts and letters; the exactness with which all the ceremonies of religion were performed; the disinterestedness, the desire of honor, the fidelity to men, and the fear of the gods, with which every father inspired his children. He could not sufficiently admire the prosperous state of the country. '*Happy*,' said he, '*is the people whom a wise king rules in such a manner.*'"

Fénelon's idyl on Crete is still more fascinating Mentor is made to say:—

"All that you will see in this wonderful island is the result of the laws of Minos. The education which the children receive renders the body healthy and robust. They are accustomed, from the first, to a frugal and laborious life; it is supposed that all the pleasures of sense enervate the body and the mind; no other pleasure is presented to them but that of being invincible by virtue, that of acquiring much glory . . . . . there *they* punish three vices which go unpunished amongst other people—ingratitude, dissimulation, and avarice. As to pomp and dissipation, there is no need to punish these, for they are unknown in Crete. . . . . . No costly furniture, no magnificent clothing, no delicious feasts, no gilded palaces are allowed."

It is thus that Mentor prepares his scholar to mould and manipulate, doubtless with the most philanthropic intentions, the people of Ithaca, and, to confirm him in these ideas, he gives him the example of Salentum.

It is thus that we receive our first political notions. We are taught to treat men very much as Oliver de Serres teaches farmers to manage and to mix the soil.

Montesquieu.—"To sustain the spirit of commerce, it is necessary that all the laws should favor it; that these same laws, by their regulations in dividing the fortunes in proportion as commerce enlarges them, should place every poor citizen in sufficiently easy circumstances to enable him to work like the others, and every rich citizen in such mediocrity that he must work, in order to retain or to acquire."

Thus the laws are to dispose of all fortunes.

"Although, in a democracy, real equality is the soul of

the State, yet it is so difficult to establish, that an extreme exactness in this matter would not always be desirable. It is sufficient that a census be established to reduce or fix the differences to a certain point. After which it is for particular laws to equalize, as it were, the inequality, by burdens imposed upon the rich, and reliefs granted to the poor."

Here, again, we see the equalization of fortunes by law, that is, by force.

"There were, in Greece, two kinds of republics. One was military, as Lacedæmon; the other commercial, as Athens. In the one it was wished (by whom?) that the citizens should be idle: in the other, the love of labor was encouraged.

"It is worth our while to pay a little attention to the extent of genius required by these legislators, that we may see how, by confounding all the virtues, they showed their wisdom to the world. Lycurgus, blending theft with the spirit of justice, the hardest slavery with extreme liberty, the most atrocious sentiments with the greatest moderation, gave stability to his city. He seemed to deprive it of all its resources, arts, commerce, money, and walls; there was ambition without the hope of rising; there were natural sentiments where the individual was neither child, nor husband, nor father. Chastity even was deprived of modesty. *By this road Sparta was led on to grandeur and to glory.*

"The phenomenon which we observe in the institutions of Greece has been seen in the midst of the *degeneracy and corruption of our modern times*. An honest legislator has formed a people where probity has appeared as natural as bravery among the Spartans. William Penn was a true Lycurgus; and although the former had peace for his object, and the latter war, they resemble each other in the singular path along which they have led *their* people, in their influence over free men, in the prejudices which they have overcome, the passions they have subdued.

"Paraguay furnishes us with another example. *Society has been accused of the crime of regarding the pleasure of commanding as the only good of life; but it will always be a noble thing to govern men by making them happy.*

"*Those who desire to form similar institutions*, will establish community of property, as in the republic of Plato; the same reverence which he enjoined for the gods, separation from strangers for the preservation of morality, and make the city and not the citizens create commerce: they should give our arts without our luxury, our wants without our desires."

Vulgar infatuation may exclaim, if it likes: "It is Montesquieu! magnificent! sublime!" I am not afraid to express my opinion, and to say: "What! you have the face to call that fine? It is frightful! it is abominable! and these extracts, which I might multiply, show that, according to Montesquieu, the persons, the liberties, the property, mankind itself, are nothing but materials to exercise the sagacity of lawgivers."

Rousseau.—Although this politician, the paramount authority of French Democracy, makes the social edifice rest upon the *general will*, no one has so completely admitted the hypothesis of the entire passiveness of human nature in the presence of the lawgiver:—

"If it is true that a great prince is a rare thing, how much more so must a great lawgiver be? The former has only to follow the pattern proposed to him by the latter. *This latter is the mechanician who invents the machine;* the former is merely the workman who sets it in motion."

And what part have men to act in all this? That of the machine, which is set in motion; or, rather, are they not the brute matter of which the machine is made? Thus, between the legislator and the prince, between the prince and his subjects, there are the same relations as those which exist between the agricultural writer and the agriculturist, the agriculturist and the clod. At what a vast height, then, is the politician placed, who rules over legislators themselves, and teaches them their trade in such imperative terms as the following:—

"Would you give consistency to the State? Bring the extremes together as much as possible. Suffer neither wealthy persons nor beggars.

"If the soil is poor and barren, or the country too much confined for the inhabitants, turn to industry and the arts, whose productions you will exchange for the provisions which you require. . . . . . On a good soil, if *you are short* of inhabitants, give all your attention to agriculture, which multiplies men, and *banish* the arts, which only serve to depopulate the country. . . . . . Pay attention to extensive and convenient coasts. *Cover the sea* with vessels, and you will have a brilliant and short existence. If your seas wash only inaccessible rocks, let the people *be barbarous,* and eat fish; they will live more quietly, perhaps better, and, most certainly, more happily. In short, besides those maxims which are common to all, every people has its own particular circumstances, which demand a legislation peculiar to itself.

"It was thus that the Hebrews formerly, and the Arabs more recently, had religion for their principal object; that of the Athenians was literature; that of Carthage and Tyre, commerce; of Rhodes, naval affairs; of Sparta, war; and of Rome, virtue. The author of the 'Spirit of Laws' has shown the art *by which the legislator should frame his institutions toward each of these objects.* . . . . . But if the legislator, mistaking his object, should take up a principle different from that which arises from the nature of things; if one should tend to slavery, and the other to liberty; if one to wealth, and the other to population; one to peace and the other to conquests; the laws will insensibly become enfeebled, the Constitution will be impaired, and the State will be subject to incessant agitations until it is destroyed, or becomes changed, and invincible Nature regains her empire."

But if nature is sufficiently invincible to *regain* its empire, why does not Rousseau admit that it had no need of the legislator to *gain* its empire from the beginning? Why does he not allow that, by obeying their own impulse, men would, of themselves, apply agriculture to a fertile district, and commerce to extensive and commodious coasts, without the interference of a Lycurgus, a Solon, or a Rousseau, who would undertake it at the risk of *deceiving themselves?*

Be that as it may, we see with what a terrible responsibility Rousseau invests inventors, institutors, conductors, and manipulators of societies.

He is, therefore, very exacting with regard to them.

"He who dares to undertake the institutions of a people ought to feel that he can, as it were, transform every individual, who is by himself a perfect and solitary whole, receiving his life and being from a larger whole of which he forms a part; he must feel that he can change the constitution of man, to fortify it, and substitute a partial and moral existence for the physical and independent one which we have all received from nature. In a word, he must deprive man of his own powers, to give him others which are foreign to him."

Poor human nature! What would become of its dignity if it were intrusted to the disciples of Rousseau?

Raynal.—" The climate, that is, the air and the soil, is the first element for the legislator. *His* resources prescribe to him his duties. First, he must consult *his* local position. A population dwelling upon maritime shores must have laws fitted for navigation. . . . . . If the colony is located in an inland region, a legislator must provide for the nature of the soil, and for its degree of fertility. . . . . .

"It is more especially in the distribution of property that the wisdom of legislation will appear. As a general rule, and in every country, when a new colony is founded, land should be given to each man sufficient for the support of his family. . . . . .

"In an uncultivated island, which *you* are colonizing with children, it will only be needful to let the germs of truth expand in the developments of reason! . . . . . But when *you* establish old people in a new country, the skill consists in *only allowing it* those injurious opinions and customs which it is impossible to cure and correct. If *you* wish to prevent them from being perpetuated, you will act upon the rising generation by a general and public education of the children. A prince, or legislator, ought never to found a colony without previously sending wise men there to instruct the youth. . . . . . In a new colony, every facility is open to the precautions of the legislator who desires *to purify the tone and the manners of the people.* If he has genius and virtue, the lands and the men which are *at his disposal* will inspire his soul with a plan of society which a writer can only vaguely trace, and in a way which would be subject to the instability of all hypotheses, which are varied and complicated by an infinity of circumstances too difficult to foresee and to combine."

One would think it was a professor of agriculture who was saying to his pupils : " The climate is the only rule for the agriculturist. *His* resources dictate to him his duties. The first thing he has to consider is his local position. If he is on a clayey soil, he must do so and so. If he has to contend with sand, this is the way in which he must set about it. Every facility is open to the agriculturist who wishes to clear and improve his soil. If he only has the skill, the manure which he has *at his disposal* will suggest to him a plan of operation, which a professor can only vaguely trace, and in a way that would be subject to the uncertainty of all hypotheses, which vary and are complicated by an infinity of circumstances too difficult to foresee and to combine."

But, oh! sublime writers, deign to remember

sometimes that this clay, this sand, this manure, of which you are disposing in so arbitrary a manner, are men, your equals, intelligent and free beings like yourselves, who have received from God, as you have, the faculty of seeing, of foreseeing, of thinking, and of judging for themselves!

Mably.—(He is supposing the laws to be worn out by time and by the neglect of security, and continues thus):—

"Under these circumstances we must be convinced that the springs of Government are relaxed. *Give them* a new tension (it is the reader who is addressed), and the evil will be remedied. . . . . . Think less of punishing the faults than of encouraging the virtues *which you want*. By this method you will bestow upon *your republic* the vigor of youth. Through ignorance of this, a free people has lost its liberty! But if the evil has made so much way that the ordinary magistrates are unable to remedy it effectually, *have recourse* to an extraordinary magistracy, whose time should be short, and its power considerable. The imagination of the citizens requires to be impressed."

In this style he goes on through twenty volumes.

There was a time when, under the influence of teaching like this, which is the root of classical education, every one was for placing himself beyond and above mankind, for the sake of arranging, organizing, and instituting it in his own way.

Condillac.—"Take upon yourself, my lord, the character

of Lycurgus or of Solon. Before you finish reading this essay, amuse yourself with giving laws to some wild people in America or in Africa. Establish these roving men in fixed dwellings; teach them to keep flocks. . . . . . Endeavor to develop the social qualities which nature has implanted in them. . . . . . Make them begin to practice the duties of humanity. . . . . . Cause the pleasures of the passions to become distasteful to them by punishments, and you will see these barbarians, with every plan of your legislation, lose a vice and gain a virtue.

"All these people have had laws. But few among them have been happy. Why is this? Because legislators have almost always been ignorant of the object of society, which is, to unite families by a common interest.

"Impartiality in law consists in two things: in establishing equality in the fortunes and in the dignity of the citizens. . . . . . In proportion to the degree of equality established by the laws, the dearer will they become to every citizen. . . . . . How can avarice, ambition, dissipation idleness, sloth, envy, hatred, or jealousy, agitate men who are equal in fortune and dignity, and to whom the laws leave no hope of disturbing their equality?

"What has been told you of the republic of Sparta ought to enlighten you on this question. No other State has had laws more in accordance with the order of nature or of equality."

It is not to be wondered at that the seventeenth and eighteenth centuries should have looked upon the human race as inert matter, ready to receive everything, form, figure, impulse, movement, and life, from a great prince, or a great legislator, or a great genius. These ages were reared in the study of antiquity, and antiquity presents everywhere, in

Egypt, Persia, Greece, and Rome, the spectacle of a few men moulding mankind according to their fancy, and mankind to this end enslaved by force or by imposture. And what does this prove? That because men and society are improvable, error, ignorance, despotism, slavery, and superstition must be more prevalent in early times. The mistake of the writers quoted above is not that they have asserted this fact, but that they have proposed it, as a rule, for the admiration and imitation of future generations. Their mistake has been, with an inconceivable absence of discernment, and upon the faith of a puerile conventionalism, that they have admitted what is inadmissible, viz., the grandeur, dignity, morality, and well-being of the artificial societies of the ancient world; they have not understood that time produces and spreads enlightenment; and that in proportion to the increase of enlightenment, right ceases to be upheld by force, and society regains possession of herself.

And, in fact, what is the political work which we are endeavoring to promote? It is no other than the instinctive effort of every people toward liberty. And what is liberty, whose name can make every heart beat, and which can agitate the world, but the union of all liberties, the liberty of conscience, of instruction, of association, of the press, of locomotion, of labor, and of exchange; in other words, the free exercise, for all, of all the inoffensive faculties; and again, in other words, the destruction of all despotisms, even of legal despotism, and the reduction of law to its only rational sphere, which is to regulate the individual right of legitimate defense, or to repress injustice.

This tendency of the human race, it must be admitted, is greatly thwarted, particularly in France, by the fatal disposition common to all politicians, of placing themselves beyond mankind, to arrange, organize, and regulate it, according to their fancy.

For whilst society is struggling to realize liberty, the great men who place themselves at its head, imbued with the principles of the seventeenth and eighteenth centuries, think only of subjecting it to the philanthropic despotism of their social inventions, and making it bear with docility, according to the expression of Rousseau, the yoke of public felicity, as pictured in their own imaginations.

This was particularly the case in France in 1789. No sooner was the old system destroyed, than society was to be submitted to other artificial arrangements, always with the same starting-point —the omnipotence of the law.

Saint Just.—"The legislator commands the future. It is for him to *will* for the good of mankind. It is for him to make men what he wishes them to be."

Robespierre.—" The function of Government is to direct the physical and moral powers of the nation toward the object of its institution."

Billaud Varennes.—" A people who are to be restored to liberty must be formed anew. Ancient prejudices must be destroyed, antiquated customs changed, depraved affections corrected, inveterate vices eradicated. For this a strong force and a vehement impulse will be necessary. . . . . Citizens, the inflexible austerity of Lycurgus created the firm basis of the Spartan republic. The feeble and trusting disposition of Solon plunged Athens into slavery. This parallel contains the whole science of Government."

Lepelletier.—" Considering the extènt of human degradation, I am convinced of the necessity of effecting an entire regeneration of the race, and, if I may so express myself, of creating a new people."

Men, therefore, are nothing but raw material. It is not for them to *will their own improvement.* They are not capable of it; according to Saint Just, it is only the legislator who is. Men are merely to be what he *wills* that they should be. According to Robespierre, who copies Rousseau literally, the legislator is to begin by assigning the aim of the *institutions of the nation.* After this, the Government has only to direct all its *physical* and *moral forces* toward this end. All this time the nation itself is to remain perfectly passive; and Billaud Varennes would teach us that it ought to have no prejudices, affections, nor wants, but such as are authorized by the legislator. He even goes so far as to say that the inflexible austerity of a man is the basis of a republic.

We have seen that, in cases where the evil is so great that the ordinary magistrates are unable to remedy it, Mably recommends a dictatorship, to promote virtue. "*Have recourse*," says he, "to an extraordinary magistracy, whose time shall be short, and his power considerable. The imagination of the people requires to be impressed." This doctrine has not been neglected. Listen to Robespierre:—

"The principle of the Republican Government is virtue, and the means to be adopted during its establishment is terror. We want to substitute, in our country, morality for egotism, probity for honor, principles for customs, duties for decorum, the empire of reason for the tyranny of fashion, contempt of vice for contempt of misfortune, pride for insolence, greatness of soul for vanity, love of glory for love of money, good people for good company, merit for intrigue, genius for wit, truth for glitter, the charm of happiness for the weariness of pleasure, the greatness of man for the littleness of the great, a magnanimous, powerful, happy people for one that is easy, frivolous, degraded; that is to say, we would substitute all the virtues and miracles of a republic for all the vices and absurdities of monarchy."

At what a vast height above the rest of mankind does Robespierre place himself here! And observe the arrogance with which he speaks. He is not content with expressing a desire for a great renovation of the human heart, he does not even expect such a result from a regular Government. No; he intends to effect it himself, and by means of terror. The object of the discourse from which this puerile and laborious mass of antithesis is extracted was, to exhibit the *principles of morality which ought to direct a revolutionary Government.* Moreover, when Robespierre asks for a dictatorship, it is not merely for the purpose of repelling a foreign enemy, or of putting down factions; it is that he may establish, by means of terror, and as a preliminary to the game of the Constitution, his own principles of morality. He pretends to nothing short of extirpating from the country, by means of terror, *egotism, honor, customs, decorum, fashion, vanity, the love of money, good company, intrigue, wit, luxury, and misery.* It is not until after he, Robespierre, shall have accomplished these *miracles,* as he rightly calls them, that he will allow the law to regain her empire. Truly, it would be well if these visionaries—who think so much of themselves and so little of mankind, who want to renew everything—would only be content with trying to reform themselves; the task would be arduous enough for them. In general, however, these gentlemen, the reformers, legislators, and politicians, do not desire to exercise an immediate despotism over mankind. No, they are too moderate and too philanthropic for that. They only contend for the despotism, the absolutism, the omnipotence of the law. They aspire only to make the law.

To show how universal this strange disposition has been in France, I had need not only to have copied the whole of the works of Mably, Raynal, Rousseau, Fénelon, and to have made long extracts from Bossuet and Montesquieu, but to have given the entire transactions of the sittings of the French Convention of 1789. I shall do no such thing, however, but merely refer the reader to them.

It is not to be wondered at that this idea should have suited Buonaparte exceedingly well. He embraced it with ardor, and put it in practice with energy. Playing the part of a chemist, Europe was to him the material for his experiments. But this material reacted against him. More than half undeceived, Buonaparte, at St. Helena, seemed to admit that there is an initiative in every people, and he became less hostile to liberty. Yet this did not prevent him from giving this lesson to his son in his will: "To govern, is to diffuse morality, education, and well-being."

After all this, I hardly need show, by fastidious quotations, the opinions of Morelly, Babeuf, Owen, Saint Simon, and Fourier. I shall confine myself to a few extracts from Louis Blanc's book on the organization of labor.

"In our project society receives the impulse of power." (Page 126.)

In what does the impulse which power gives to society consist? In imposing upon it the *project* of M. Louis Blanc.

On the other hand, society is the human race. The human race, then, is to receive its impulse from M. Louis Blanc.

It is at liberty to do so or not, it will be said. Of course the human race is at liberty to take advice from anybody, whoever it may be. But this is not the way in which M. Louis Blanc understands the thing. He means that his project should be converted into *law*, and, consequently, forcibly imposed by power.

"In our project the State has only to give a legislation to labor, by means of which the industrial movement may and ought to be accomplished *in all liberty*. It (the State) merely places society on an incline (*that is all*) that it may descend, when once it is placed there, by the mere force of things, and by the natural course of the *established mechanism*."

But what is this incline? One indicated by M. Louis Blanc. Does it not lead to an abyss? No, it leads to happiness. Why, then, does not society go there of itself? Because it does not know what it wants, and it requires an impulse. What is to give it this impulse? Power. And who is to give the impulse to power? The inventor of the machine, M. Louis Blanc.

We shall never get out of this circle—mankind passive, and a great man moving it by the intervention of the law.

Once on this incline, will society enjoy something like liberty? Without a doubt. And what is liberty?

"Once for all, liberty consists, not only in the right granted, but in the power given to man, to exercise, to develop his faculties under the empire of justice, and under the protection of the law.

"And this is no vain distinction; there is a deep meaning in it, and its consequences are not to be estimated. For when once it is admitted that man, to be truly free, must have the power to exercise and develop his faculties, it follows that every member of society has a claim upon it for such instruction as shall *enable* it to display itself, and for the instruments of labor, without which human activity can find no scope. Now, by whose intervention is society to give to each of its members the requisite instruction and the necessary instruments of labor, unless by that of the State?"

Thus, liberty is power. In what does this power consist? In possessing instruction and instruments of labor. Who is to give instruction and instruments of labor? Society, *who owes them*. By whose intervention is society to give instruments of labor to those who do not possess them? By the *intervention of the State*. From whom is the State to obtain them?

It is for the reader to answer this question, and to notice whither all this tends.

One of the strangest phenomena of our time, and one which will probably be a matter of astonishment to our descendants, is the doctrine which is founded upon this triple hypothesis: the radical passiveness of mankind, the omnipotence of the law, the infallibility of the legislator; this is the sacred symbol of the party which proclaims itself exclusively democratic.

It is true that it professes also to be *social*.

So far as it is democratic, it has an unlimited faith in mankind.

So far as it is social, it places it beneath the mud.

Are political rights under discussion? Is a legislator to be chosen? Oh! then the people possess science by instinct; they are gifted with an admirable tact; *their will is always right;* the general *will cannot err.* Suffrage cannot be too *universal.* Nobody is under any responsibility to society. The will and the capacity to choose well are taken for granted. Can the people be mistaken? Are we not living in an age of enlightenment? What! are the people to be always kept in leading-strings? Have they not acquired their rights at the cost of effort and sacrifice? Have they not given sufficient proof of intelligence and wisdom? Are they not arrived at maturity? Are they not in a state to judge for themselves? Do they not know their own interest? Is there a man or a class who would dare to claim the right of putting himself in the place of the people, of deciding and of acting for them? No, no; the people would be *free*, and they shall be so. They wish to conduct their own affairs, and they shall do so.

But when once the legislator is duly elected, then indeed the style of his speech alters. The nation is sent back into passiveness, inertness, nothingness, and the legislator takes possession of omnipotence. It is for him to invent, for him to direct, for him to impel, for him to organize. Mankind has nothing to do but to submit; the hour of despotism has struck. And we must observe that this is decisive; for the people, just before so enlightened, so moral, so perfect, have no inclinations at all, or, if they have any, they all lead them downwards toward degradation. And yet they ought to have a little liberty! But are we not assured, by M. Considerant, that *liberty leads fatally to monopoly?* Are we not told that liberty is competition, and that competition, according to M. Louis Blanc, *is a system of extermination for the people, and of ruination for trade?* For that reason people are exterminated and ruined in proportion as they are free; take, for example, Switzerland, Holland, England, and the United States! Does not M. Louis Blanc tell us again that *competition leads to monopoly, and that, for the same reason, cheapness leads to exorbitant prices?* That *competition tends to drain the sources of consumption, and urges production to a destructive activity?* That *competition forces production to increase, and consumption to decrease?* whence it follows that free people produce for the sake of not consuming; that there is nothing but *oppression and madness* among them; and that it is absolutely necessary for M. Louis Blanc to see to it!

What sort of liberty should be allowed to men? Liberty of conscience? But we should see them all profiting by the permission to become atheists. Liberty of education? But parents would be paying professors to teach their sons immorality and error; besides, if we are to believe M. Thiers, education, if left to the national liberty, would cease to be national, and we should be educating our children in the ideas of the Turks or Hindoos, instead of which they have the good fortune to be educated in the noble ideas of the Romans. Liberty of labor? But this is only competition, whose effect is to leave all productions unconsumed, to exterminate the people, and to ruin the tradesmen. The liberty of exchange? But it is well known that the protectionists have shown, over and over again, that a man must be ruined when he exchanges freely, and that to become rich it is necessary to exchange without liberty. Liberty of association? But, according to the socialist doctrine, liberty and association exclude each other, for the liberty of men is attacked just to force them to associate.

You must see, then, that the socialist democrats cannot in conscience allow men any liberty, because, by their own nature, they tend in every instance to all kinds of degradation and demoralization.

We are therefore left to conjecture, in this case, upon what foundation universal suffrage is claimed for them with so much importunity.

The pretensions of organizers suggest another question, which I have often asked them, and to which I am not aware that I ever received an answer: Since the natural tendencies of mankind are so bad that it is not safe to allow them liberty, how comes it to pass that the tendencies of organizers are always good? Do not the legislators and their agents form a part of the human race? Do they consider that they are composed of different materials from the rest of mankind? They say that society, when left to itself, rushes to inevitable destruction, because its instincts are perverse. They pretend to stop it in its downward course, and to give it a better direction. They have, therefore, received from heaven intelligence and virtues which place them beyond and above mankind. Let them show their title to this superiority. They would be our shepherds, and we are to be their flock. This arrangement presupposes in them a natural superiority, the right to which we are fully justified in calling upon them to prove.

You must observe that I am not contending against their right to invent social combinations, to propagate them, to recommend them, and to try them upon themselves, at their own expense and risk; but I do dispute their right to impose them upon us through the medium of the law, that is, by force and by public taxes.

I would not insist upon the Cabetists, the Fourierists, the Proudhonians, the Universitaries, and the Protectionists renouncing their own particular ideas; I would only have them renounce that idea which is common to them all—viz., that of subjecting us by force to their own groups and series, to their social workshops, to their bank for lending money without interest, to their Græco-Romano morality, and to their commercial restrictions. I would ask them to allow us the faculty of judging of their plans, and not to oblige us to adopt them, if we find that they hurt our interests or are repugnant to our consciences.

To presume to have recourse to power and taxation, besides being oppressive and unjust, implies, further, the injurious supposition that the organizer is infallible, and mankind incompetent.

And if mankind is not competent to judge for itself, why do they talk so much about universal suffrage?

This contradiction in ideas is unhappily to be found also in facts; and whilst the French nation has claimed precedence over all others in obtaining its rights, or rather its political claims, this has by no means prevented it from being more governed, and directed, and imposed upon, and fettered, and cheated, than any other nation. It is also the one, of all others, where revolutions are constantly to be dreaded, and it is perfectly natural that it should be so.

So long as this idea is retained, which is admitted by all our politicians, and so energetically expressed by M. Louis Blanc in these words, "Society receives its impulse from power;" so long as men consider themselves as capable of feeling, yet passive; incapable of raising themselves by their own discernment and by their own energy to any morality or well-being, while they expect everything from the law; in a word, while they admit that their relations with the State are the same as those of the flock with the shepherd, it is clear that the responsibility of power is immense. Fortune and misfortune, wealth and destitution, equality and inequality, all proceed from it. It is charged with everything, it undertakes everything, it does everything; therefore it has to answer for everything. If we are happy, it has a right to claim our gratitude; but if we are miserable, it alone must bear the blame. Are not our persons and property, in fact, at its disposal? Is not the law omnipotent? In regulating industry, it has engaged to make it prosper, otherwise it would have been absurd to deprive it of its liberty; and if it suffers, whose fault is it? In pretending to adjust the balance of commerce by the game of tariffs, it engages to make it prosper; and if, so far from prospering, it is destroyed, whose fault is it? In granting its protection to maritime instrumentalities in exchange for free navigation, it has engaged to render them lucrative; if these restrictions become burdensome, whose fault is it?

Thus, there is not a grievance in the nation for which the Government does not voluntarily make itself responsible. Is it to be wondered at that every failure threatens to cause a revolution?

And what is the remedy proposed? To extend indefinitely the dominion of the law, *i.e.*, the responsibility of Government. But if the Government engages to raise and to regulate wages, and is not able to do it; if it engages to assist all those who are in want, and is not able to do it; if it engages to provide an asylum for every laborer, and is not able to do it; if it engages to offer to all such as are eager to borrow, gratuitous credit, and is not able to do it; if, in words which we regret should have escaped the pen of M. de Lamartine, "the State considers that its mission is to enlighten, to develop, to enlarge, to strengthen, to spiritualize, and to sanctify the soul of the people," —if it fails in this, is it not evident that after every disappointment, which, alas! is more than probable, there will be a no less inevitable revolution?

I shall now resume the subject by remarking that immediately after the economical part * of the question, and at the entrance of the political part, a leading question presents itself. It is the following:—

What is law? What ought it to be? What is its domain? What are its limits? Where, in fact, does the prerogative of the legislator stop?

I have no hesitation in answering, *Law is common force organized to prevent injustice;* in short, Law is Justice.

---

* Political economy precedes politics: the former has to discover whether human interests are harmonious or antagonistic, a fact which must have been decided upon before politics can determine the prerogatives of Government.

It is not true that the legislator has absolute power over our persons and property, since they pre-exist, and his work is only to secure them from injury.

It is not true that the mission of the law is to regulate our consciences, our ideas, our will, our education, our sentiments, our works, our exchanges, our gifts, our enjoyments. Its mission is to prevent the rights of one from interfering with those of another in any one of these things.

Law, because it has force for its necessary sanction, can only have as its lawful domain the domain of force, which is justice.

And as every individual has a right to have recourse to force only in cases of lawful defense, so collective force, which is only the union of individual forces, cannot be rationally used for any other end.

The law, then, is solely the organization of individual rights, which existed before legitimate defense.

Law is justice.

So far from being able to oppress the persons of the people, or to plunder their property, even for a philanthropic end, its mission is to protect the former, and to secure to them the possession of the latter.

It must not be said, either, that it may be philanthropic, so long as it abstains from all oppression; for this is a contradiction. The law cannot avoid acting upon our persons and property; if it does not secure them, it violates them if it touches them.

The law is justice.

Nothing can be more clear and simple, more perfectly defined and bounded, or more visible to every eye; for justice is a given quantity, immutable and unchangeable, and which admits of neither *increase* nor *diminution*.

Depart from this point, make the law religious, fraternal, equalizing, industrial, literary, or artistic, and you will be lost in vagueness and uncertainty; you will be upon unknown ground, in a forced Utopia, or, which is worse, in the midst of a multitude of Utopias, striving to gain possession of the law, and to impose it upon you; for fraternity and philanthropy have no fixed limits, like justice. Where will you stop? Where is the law to stop? One person will only extend his philanthropy to some of the industrial classes, and will require the law to *influence the consumers in favor of the producers*. Another, like M. Considerant, will take up the cause of the working classes, and claim for them by means of the law, at a fixed rate, *clothing, lodging, food, and everything necessary for the support of life*. A third, as M. Louis Blanc, will say, and with reason, that this would be an incomplete fraternity, and that the law ought to provide them with instruments of labor and the means of instruction. A fourth will observe that such an arrangement still leaves room for inequality, and that the law ought to introduce into the most remote hamlets luxury, literature, and the arts. This is the high road to communism; in other words, legislation will be—what it now is—the battle-field for everybody's dreams and everybody's covetousness.

Law is justice.

In this proposition we represent to ourselves a simple, immovable Government. And I defy any one to tell me whence the thought of a revolution, an insurrection, or a simple disturbance could arise against a public force confined to the repression of injustice. Under such a system there would be more well-being, and this well-being would be more equally distributed; and as to the sufferings inseparable from humanity, no one would think of accusing the Government of them, for it would be as innocent of them as it is of the variations of the temperature. Have the people ever been known to rise against the court of appeals, or assail the justices of the peace, for the sake of claiming the rate of wages, gratuitous credit, instruments of labor, the advantages of the tariff, or the social workshop? They know perfectly well that these combinations are beyond the jurisdiction of the justices of the peace, and they would soon learn that they are not within the jurisdiction of the law.

But if the law were to be made upon the principle of fraternity, if it were to be proclaimed that from it proceed all benefits and all evils, that it is responsible for every individual grievance and for every social inequality, then you open the door to an endless succession of complaints, irritations, troubles, and revolutions.

Law is justice.

And it would be very strange if it could properly be anything else! Is not justice right? Are not rights equal? With what show of right can the law interfere to subject me to the social plans of Smith, Jones, and Robinson, rather than to subject these gentlemen to *my* plans? Is it to be supposed that nature has not bestowed upon ME sufficient imagination to invent a Utopia too? Is it for the law to make choice of one amongst so many fancies, and to make use of the public force in its service?

Law is justice.

And let it not be said, as it continually is, that the law, in this sense, would be atheistic, individual, and heartless, and that it would make mankind wear its own image. This is an absurd conclusion, quite worthy of the governmental infatuation which sees mankind in the law.

What then? Does it follow, that if we are free, we shall cease to act? Does it follow, that if we do not receive an impulse from the law, we shall receive no impulse at all? Does it follow, that if the law confines itself to securing to us the free exercise of our faculties, our faculties will be paralyzed? Does it follow, that if the law does not impose upon us forms of religion, modes of association, methods of instruction, rules for labor, directions for exchange, and plans for charity, we shall plunge eagerly into atheism, isolation, ignorance, misery, and egotism? Does it follow, that we shall no longer recognize the power and goodness of God; that we shall cease to associate together, to help each other, to love and assist our unfortunate brethren, to study the secrets of nature, and to aspire after perfection in our existence?

Law is justice.

And it is under the law of justice, under the reign of right, under the influence of liberty, security, stability, and responsibility, that every man will attain to the measure of his worth, to all the dignity of his being, and that mankind will accomplish, with order and with calmness—slowly, it is true, but with certainty—the progress decreed to it.

I believe that my theory is correct; for whatever be the question upon which I am arguing, whether it be religious, philosophical, political, or economical; whether it affects well-being, morality, equality, right, justice, progress, responsibility, property, labor, exchange, capital, wages, taxes, population, credit, or Government; at whatever point of the scientific horizon I start from, I invariably come to the same thing—the solution of the social problem is in liberty.

And have I not experience on my side? Cast your eye over the globe. Which are the happiest, the most moral, and the most peaceable nations? Those where the law interferes the least with private activity; where the Government is the least felt; where individuality has the most scope, and public opinion the most influence; where the machinery of the administration is the least important and the least complicated; where taxation is lightest and least unequal, popular discontent the least excited and the least justifiable; where the responsibility of individuals and classes is the most active, and where, consequently, if morals are not in a perfect state, at any rate they tend incessantly to correct themselves; where transactions, meetings, and associations are the least fettered; where labor, capital, and production suffer the least from artificial displacements; where mankind follows most completely its own natural course; where the thought of God prevails the most over the inventions of men; those, in short, who realize the most nearly this idea: That, within the limits of right, all human transactions should flow from the free, perfectible, and voluntary action of man; nothing be attempted by the law or by force, except the administration of universal justice.

I cannot avoid coming to this conclusion—that there are too many great men in the world; there are too many legislators, organizers, institutors of society, conductors of the people, fathers of nations, etc., etc. Too many persons place themselves above mankind, to rule and patronize it; too many persons make a trade of attending to it. It will be answered: "You yourself are occupied upon it all this time." Very true. But it must be admitted that it is in another sense entirely that I am speaking; and if I join the reformers, it is solely for the purpose of inducing them to relax their hold.

I am not doing as the inventor Vaucauson did with his automaton, but as a physiologist does with the organization of the human frame; I would study and admire it.

I am acting with regard to it in the spirit which

animated a celebrated traveler. He found himself in the midst of a savage tribe. A child had just been born, and a crowd of soothsayers, magicians, and quacks were around it, armed with rings, hooks, and bandages. One said, "This child will never smell the perfume of a calumet, unless I stretch his nostrils." Another said, "He will be without the sense of hearing, unless I draw his ears down to his shoulders." A third said, "He will never see the light of the sun, unless I give his eyes an oblique direction." A fourth said, "He will never be upright, unless I bend his legs." A fifth said, "He will not be able to think, unless I press his brain." "Stop!" said the traveler. "Whatever God does is well done; do not pretend to know more than He; and as He has given organs to this frail creature, allow those organs to develop themselves, to strengthen themselves by exercise, use, experience, and liberty."

God has implanted in mankind, also, all that is necessary to enable it to accomplish its destinies. There is a providential social physiology, as well as a providential human physiology. The social organs are constituted so as to enable them to develop harmoniously in the grand air of liberty. Away, then, with quacks and organizers! Away with their rings, and their chains, and their hooks, and their pincers! Away with their artificial methods! Away with their social workshops, their governmental whims, their centralization, their tariffs, their State universities, their State religions, their banks to lend gratuitously to everybody, their limitations, their restrictions, their moralizations, and their equalization by taxation! And now, after having vainly inflicted upon the social body so many systems, let them end where they ought to have begun: reject all systems, and make trial of liberty—of liberty, which is an act of faith in God and in His work.

Works on Political Economy.

1. **THE WEALTH OF NATIONS,** an enquiry into the Nature and Causes of, by ADAM SMITH. 12mo, cloth extra, 792 pages.....$2 25

    A perennial work, and the only book in history to which has been accorded the honor of a Centenary Celebration.

2. **ESSAYS ON POLITICAL ECONOMY.** By FREDERICK BASTIAT, with Introduction and Notes by DAVID A. WELLS. 12mo, cloth, $1 25

    "The laws of an abstruse science have never been made more clear, or expressed more forcibly."—*Cincinnati Commercial.*

3. **THE SOPHISMS OF PROTECTION.** By FREDERICK BASTIAT, with Introduction by HORACE WHITE. 12mo, cloth extra, 400 pages........................$1 00

    "Contains the most telling statements of the leading principles of Free-Trade ever published."—*N. Y. Nation.*

4. **WHAT IS FREE-TRADE?** An adaptation for American Readers of Bastiat's "Sophisms of Protection." By EMILE WALTER, a Worker. 12mo, cloth.................... 75

    "Unsurpassed in the happiness of its illustrations."—*N. Y. Nation.*

5. **SOCIAL ECONOMY.** By Prof. J. E. THOROLD ROGERS. Revised and edited for American readers. 12mo, cloth.................... 75

    "Gives in the compass of 150 pages, concise, yet comprehensive answers to the most important questions in social economy * * * cannot be too highly recommended for the use of teachers, students, and the general public."—*American Athenæum.*

6. **PROTECTION AND FREE-TRADE.** A Series of Essays. By ISAAC BUTTS. 12mo, cloth extra..................$1 25

    "A clear and effective presentation of the case."—*N. Y. Evening Post.*

7. **AN ALPHABET IN FINANCE.** A simple statement of permanent principles, and their application to questions of the day. By GRAHAM MCADAM. With Introduction by R. R. BOWKER. 12mo, cloth $1 25

    "A timely volume, whose directness and raciness can but be of service."—*New Englander.*
    "A model of clear-thinking and happy expression."—*Portland Press.*

G. P. PUTNAM'S SONS,
182 Fifth Avenue, N. Y.

PUTNAM'S SERIES OF ATLASES.

I. **NEW MERCANTILE MAP OF THE WORLD, on Mercator's Projection.** For Merchants, Shippers, Ship Owners, etc. Size, 55x40 inches. Price, in cloth, or on rollers, $10.00.

II. **THE INTERNATIONAL ATLAS.** POLITICAL, CLASSICAL, AND HISTORICAL, consisting of 62 Maps—32 of Modern Geography, showing all the latest Discoveries and changes of Boundaries, and 30 of Historical and Classical Geography, with descriptive Letter-press of Historical and Classical Geography, by WM. F. COLLIER, LL.D., and LEONARD SCHMITZ, LL.D., with copious Indices. 8vo, cloth extra, $6.00.

III. **THE COLLEGIATE ATLAS.** A new, comprehensive and useful Atlas of Modern Geography for the Library and for ordinary reference, with about 40 Maps. 1872. Imp. 8vo, cloth extra, $4.00.

IV. **THE STUDENT'S ATLAS of PHYSICAL GEOGRAPHY.** Consisting of 20 Maps with descriptive Letter-press, illustrated by numerous engravings. Imp. 8vo, cloth extra, $2.50.

V. **THE STUDENT'S ATLAS OF HISTORICAL AND CLASSICAL GEOGRAPHY.** (The two above works bound together.) Containing 30 Maps, with descriptive Letter-press. Cloth, $2.50.

VI. **THE STUDENT'S ATLAS OF CLASSICAL GEOGRAPHY.** Containing 15 Maps, Imperial 8vo; with descriptive Letter-press, by L. SCHMITZ, LL.D. Cloth, $1.50.

VII. **THE STUDENT'S ATLAS OF HISTORICAL GEOGRAPHY.** Consisting of 16 Maps, Imperial 8vo; constructed and engraved by Miller, with descriptive Letter-press, by WM. F. COLLIER, LL.D., and full Index. Cloth, $1.50.

VIII. **THE PORTABLE ATLAS of MODERN GEOGRAPHY.** Constructed and Engraved by JOHN BARTHOLOMEW, F.R.A.S. With 16 Maps. Imperial 8vo. Cloth, $1.00.

IX. **THE ATLAS OF SCRIPTURE GEOGRAPHY.** 16 Maps, with Questions with each Map. Small quarto, cloth, 75 cents.

Some few of the CRITICISMS *on* "PUTNAM'S SERIES OF ATLASES."

"The INTERNATIONAL ATLAS . . . is handsome and accurate, beautifully engraved, and exquisitely colored . . . of exceptional completeness."—*N. Y. Evening Mail.*

"The Maps are well executed, and the work is most convenient for reference."—*N. Y. Tribune.*

"The Maps of the CLASSICAL ATLAS are of exquisite clearness and beauty."—*Christian Union.*

"The Maps of the PORTABLE ATLAS are excellent, and the series to which it belongs contains the best low-priced Atlases in the market."—*N. Y. Ev. Mail.*

"The SCRIPTURE ATLAS is full, accurate, clear, and portable."—*Christian Union.*

"We refer to it with edification and delight."—*Rhode Island Schoolmaster.*

"A very complete and compendious work, apparently accurate and in beautiful style."—*Rev. Stephen H. Tyng, D.D.*

G. P. PUTNAM'S SONS, New York.

www.ingramcontent.com/pod-product-compliance
Lightning Source LLC
Chambersburg PA
CBHW022026240426
43667CB00042B/1202